Gaining Personal Financial Freedom

through the Biblical Principles of Finances

Larry A. Maxwell

Church Growth Institute

Providing Practical Tools for Growth
P.O. Box 4404, Lynchburg, VA 24502

Editor: Cindy G. Spear
Designer: Carolyn Reichard
Editorial & Design Assistant: Tamara Johnson

Table of Contents

INTRODUCTION

Welcome to a practical look at *The Biblical Principles of Finances*. As you read through this material you will embark on a study of what the Bible says about you and your finances. This study may be unlike any other study of finances you have ever undertaken. It centers on *living* rather than *giving*. It is filled with practical application of biblical principles to daily living.

Be sure to approach this material with a careful, prayerful attitude. Look up each Scripture reference and read it in light of both its immediate and overall context. Some of the principles may be new to you, but they are as old as the Word of God.

You will look at the financial test you are involved in every day and find out how to pass it.

You will examine God's standard for your life and discover how understanding that standard can bring you great peace.

You will see God's order in finances. You will realize that if you learn to apply God's order in finances to your personal finances, you will find His blessing in your financial undertakings.

You will look at the joy of debt-free living and discover the steps to attaining it. You will see practical steps which can help you get out of debt and stay out of debt.

You will realize the benefits of having a written budget, built upon God's principles and will see how to put together a budget that really works. You will discover how to use "The Christian Budget Bookkeeping System," a system that is easy to maintain.

You will explore the biblical teaching regarding abundance and how God desires to make you abound in the area of finances.

You will learn how to be a wise steward in handling your savings and investments. You will also see practical principles regarding insurance and inheritances.

You should not have any misunderstanding about what the Bible has to say about money when you finish this study.

Applying the biblical principles of finances to your life requires **wisdom** and **discipline**, but God will help you if you ask Him (James 1:2-12).

You can experience an exhilarating freedom when you learn to apply God's principles to your life. If you are handling your finances according to the biblical principles of finances, I encourage you to study this material and use it to help others experience the financial freedom you have come to know.

I am especially thankful to Larry Coy, who taught me the importance of applying biblical principles to my life, and who drilled into me the principle of not borrowing, and of staying out of debt no matter how tough the situation. To Rebekah my faithful wife, who knows what it is to see these principles put to the test in daily living. To Larry Burkett, whose teaching and materials on finances helped me to organize many of these thoughts. To the good people in the churches I pastored, and to the students I have taught in college and seminary who patiently listened and applied these principles to their lives, and who are a living testimony of their validity and effectiveness. And to Him who caused all the events and people to come into my life, so He could teach me His principles to share with you (2 Tim. 2:2).

As an *accountant* and *salesman*, I found that these principles work in business. As a *teacher* and *administrator*, I found that they work in education. As a *pastor* and *evangelist* I found that they work in ministry. And as a *husband* and *father* of four children, I have found that they work in the home. I know they will work for you.

Before you proceed any further please take a moment and fill out the following **Personal Financial Information Review** – a questionnaire that will help you see how well you understand the biblical principles of finances before you begin this study. The first section contains questions based on the Word of God and are unchangeable. The second section contains questions based on our financial and monetary system which does change as the economy changes. I think you'll find the questionnaire interesting. One word of caution, don't answer the questions too quickly. Some of them are worded in such a way that a quick answer will probably be wrong, so give them a little thought.

After you fill out the **Personal Financial Information Review** check your answers with the answer key, then proceed with your study of *The Biblical Principles of Finances*.

May God add His blessings to you as you begin this study.

The Biblical Principles of Finances
PERSONAL FINANCIAL INFORMATION REVIEW

Part One: Biblical Principles
[Answer each question *True* or *False*]
This section will help you to see how well you understand some of the biblical principles of finances.

T F

☐ ☐ 1. Finances are a spiritual matter.

☐ ☐ 2. Money is the root of all evil.

☐ ☐ 3. It is wrong to go in debt.

☐ ☐ 4. You should not cosign a loan.

☐ ☐ 5. You should only use your home as collateral.

☐ ☐ 6. Investing and receiving interest is wrong.

☐ ☐ 7. Loaning to other believers with interest is wrong.

☐ ☐ 8. Christians should not have a savings account.

☐ ☐ 9. We are responsible to feed the poor.

☐ ☐ 10. Christians should loan to a brother in need.

☐ ☐ 11. The main deciding factor when choosing between two jobs should be, which one provides the best financial security?

☐ ☐ 12. The Bible says some about giving but little about other financial matters.

☐ ☐ 13. The "firstfruits principle," or tithe, is expected of all Jews and Christians.

☐ ☐ 14. The tithe is whatever offering we decide to give to God.

☐ ☐ 15. Family needs must always come before anything else.

T   F

☐   ☐   16. A truly spiritual Christian will never be financially prosperous.

☐   ☐   17. God expects grandparents to leave an inheritance to their grandchildren.

☐   ☐   18. All Christian heads-of-households should have some form of insurance.

☐   ☐   19. The church is expected to take care of all its widows.

☐   ☐   20. Not reporting "under the table" business dealings is sin.

☐   ☐   21. Christians should not use all the deductions they can use on their taxes.

☐   ☐   22. A Christian does not have to pay taxes.

☐   ☐   23. A person who does not work, when they can, should be allowed to go hungry.

☐   ☐   24. Every Christian who walks close to God can expect to own their own home.

☐   ☐   25. The two things we can always expect God to provide for us are food and clothing.

☐   ☐   26. God wants all believers to have their finances in order so He can bless them and they will be able to give when valid needs arise.

☐   ☐   27. God expects us to have some order or system by which we take care of our finances.

☐   ☐   28. Christians do not have to work hard for their employers because God is their only boss.

☐   ☐   29. We should pray about every financial expenditure.

☐   ☐   30. Our main effort in life should be to establish financial security.

T   F

☐   ☐   31. It is wrong to gamble or play the lottery.

☐   ☐   32. God expects us to get out of debt before we spend money on things we want.

☐   ☐   33. Money or work will try to take priority over your spiritual or family life.

☐   ☐   34. God blesses in proportion to our giving.

☐   ☐   35. God provides us with an abundance so we can help others.

☐   ☐   36. God's people can borrow from others but not lend.

☐   ☐   37. We do not have to pay all of our debts.

☐   ☐   38. To not give God at least 10 percent of all your income will eventually bring you financial and spiritual ruin.

☐   ☐   39. Pride is one of the greatest obstacles to getting our finances in order.

☐   ☐   40. Christians should not claim bankruptcy.

Part Two: Financial Principles
[Answer each question *True* or *False*]
This section will help you to see how well you understand some basic financial principles.

T   F

☐   ☐   41. The Passbook Savings Account is always the best place to invest your money.

☐   ☐   42. A bank is the safest place to keep your money.

☐   ☐   43. You must have at least $10,000 before you can consider getting any real return on your money.

☐   ☐   44. Investments returning over 30 percent are available to investors with as little as $1,000 to invest.

T   F

☐   ☐   45. Life insurance agents are the best people to get advice from regarding life insurance.

☐   ☐   46. Whole life, variable life, and paid-up life insurance have comparatively low returns for your investment dollar.

☐   ☐   47. Investing money is too difficult for the average person to understand.

☐   ☐   48. Many banks have free checking accounts to those who maintain a balance of $500 in their account.

☐   ☐   49. A bank is the best place to go for financial advice.

☐   ☐   50. Many banks pay interest on checking accounts with a minimum balance of $100.

☐   ☐   51. Credit cards are the financial downfall of many people.

☐   ☐   52. Buying a house always makes more financial sense than renting a house or apartment.

☐   ☐   53. Avoid consolidation loans.

☐   ☐   54. An IRA (Individual Retirement Account) can be a very good investment.

☐   ☐   55. The penalties on withdrawing money from an IRA are so high, you should never consider doing it.

☐   ☐   56. An IRA can be opened for as little as $50.

☐   ☐   57. Find one good IRA and leave your money in it until you retire. Do not switch between funds.

☐   ☐   58. Investing in stocks is always risky.

☐   ☐   59. People who do not understand stocks should not invest in them.

T F

☐ ☐ 60. Mutual Funds are a good means of investing for the small investor.

☐ ☐ 61. All investments have heavy fees connected with them.

☐ ☐ 62. Penny stocks have one of the highest rates of return for the small investor.

☐ ☐ 63. You may claim more exemptions than you have to be deducted from your paycheck by your employer.

☐ ☐ 64. You may claim more exemptions on your income taxes than you have.

☐ ☐ 65. Sheltering income from taxes is illegal and unspiritual.

☐ ☐ 66. Ten percent compounded interest would produce a greater return for the same investment period than 10 percent simple interest.

☐ ☐ 67. If you die without a will your family may negotiate how your entire estate is handled.

☐ ☐ 68. Funeral plans and expenses should be considered before you die.

☐ ☐ 69. As a general rule of thumb children should not be insured.

☐ ☐ 70. No one earns too little or too much to have a written budget.

☐ ☐ 71. Gold is the most stable investment you can make.

☐ ☐ 72. Utility company budget plans are the best plan to use for paying your utility bills.

☐ ☐ 73. Different banks in the same area offer different rates on mortgages.

T   F

☐   ☐   74. It is best to do all your banking with one bank.

☐   ☐   75. It is always best to have a tax preparer do you taxes.

☐   ☐   76. Self-employed people need to figure an estimated yearly income and expense profile, then figure a budget and pay themselves a regular weekly or monthly amount.

☐   ☐   77. It is not important to keep financial records.

☐   ☐   78. If audited by the Internal Revenue Service (IRS), you must prove every expense and deduction claimed.

☐   ☐   79. The IRS has its own courts and does not require a jury to sit when deciding on your tax case.

☐   ☐   80. It is important to keep informed financially.

Part Three: Personal Evaluation
[Answer each question *Yes* or *No*]
This section will help you to see how well you are applying the biblical principles of finances to your life.

Y   N

☐   ☐   81. Do you faithfully give God the tithe (firstfruits)?

☐   ☐   82. Do you have a written budget that you stick by?

☐   ☐   83. Do you have a retirement plan?

☐   ☐   84. Do you have a written plan that provides for your family in the event of your death?

☐   ☐   85. Have you written some tentative funeral plans?

☐   ☐   86. Did you, or are you, teaching your children how to tithe?

☐   ☐   87. Did you, or are you, teaching your children how to budget and save?

Y   N

☐   ☐ 88. Are you teaching your family that God comes first by faithfully giving Him the tithe?

☐   ☐ 89. Are you teaching your family that God provides by providing them adequate food and clothing before debt payments, before wants, and before housing expenses?

☐   ☐ 90. Are you teaching your family that God wants to bless them by providing them with wants, before getting for yourself?

☐   ☐ 91. Are you obeying God's command to stay out of debt?

☐   ☐ 92. Are you obeying Proverbs 27:1 and not buying things by anticipating future income to pay for them?

☐   ☐ 93. Are you allowing God to provide by praying before purchasing your wants or needs?

☐   ☐ 94. Do you pray daily for God to provide your daily bread?

☐   ☐ 95. Did you choose your current job on the basis that it is the one that allows you to serve God most effectively?

☐   ☐ 96. Do you regularly give God an offering, above the tithe?

☐   ☐ 97. Have you recently made a faith promise to God?

☐   ☐ 98. Do you have an emergency fund equal to three months take-home pay?

☐   ☐ 99. Are you currently setting money aside for savings?

☐   ☐ 100. If you could not answer "Yes" to questions 81 through 99, are you willing to make any changes in the way you handle your finances based on biblical principles?

Answers
Part One – Biblical Principles

1. True	15. False	29. True
2. False	16. False	30. False
3. True	17. True	31. True
4. True	18. True	32. True
5. False	19. False	33. True
6. False	20. True	34. True
7. True	21. False	35. True
8. False	22. False	36. False
9. True	23. True	37. False
10. False	24. False	38. True
11. False	25. True	39. True
12. False	26. True	40. True
13. True	27. True	
14. False	28. False	

Part Two – Financial Principles

41. False	55. False	69. True
42. False	56. True	70. True
43. False	57. False	71. False
44. True	58. True	72. False
45. False	59. False	73. True
46. True	60. True	74. False
47. False	61. False	75. False
48. True	62. False	76. True
49. False	63. True	77. False
50. True	64. False	78. True
51. True	65. False	79. True
52. False	66. True	80. True
53. True	67. False	
54. True	68. True	

Part Three – Personal Evaluation

(Answers will vary with each individual.)

Chapter One
WILL YOU PASS THE FINANCIAL TEST?

You May Not Realize It, But You Are Taking a Test

One day I conducted a survey and asked high school students what they liked least about school. Overwhelmingly the thing they said they liked least about school was taking tests.

High school students are not alone in their distaste for tests. Most people feel a certain amount of anxiety when they have to take a test. If they know a test is coming, some people will stay up late the night before a test, so they can cram as much information into their head as possible, hoping it will help them get a better grade.

When people are placed in a situation where they know they are going to be tested, everyone wants to do well. That takes preparation. I'll never forget walking into class one day to discover that the teacher was giving a major test which I had forgotten all about. What an awful feeling that was. I was totally unprepared and my grade clearly reflected that fact.

Most people would prefer all tests to be given in a classroom and to know when they are going to be tested. But all tests are not given in the classroom. In fact most tests take place outside of the classroom.

We are being tested every day. The supervisor at work evaluates the employee's performance. The inspector carefully checks the finished products on the assembly line. The police officer waits along the side of the road to see if passing motorists abide by the law. All of these are tests. Every day, in many different ways, we are subjected to testing either formally or informally. Often we do not even realize it.

The Bible tells us there is another type of test we take each day. It is a practical hands-on test, conducted so subtly you may not even realize it is a test. More people fail than pass this test. *It is the test of how you handle your finances.* Though no one is standing over you to pass out a grade, the results of how you handle the financial test will affect you physically, emotionally, and spiritually. It is conducted daily in the classroom of life, every time you handle finances.

All throughout the day, either consciously or unconsciously you handle finances. Even as you read this book you are either spending money or earning money. You could be earning money by deciding to apply the principles you will learn. That decision can save you hundreds of dollars and show you how to use the money you have more wisely. Or you could be spending money in very simple ways which we often take for granted. For example, if you are using a lamp to provide light to read this book, that lamp is using electricity and that electricity is costing money. Is the temperature in your room regulated? Heating and cooling a room costs money too. The clothing you are wearing right now is being soiled just by the fact you are wearing it. It will have to be washed, which will also cost money. As you sit there you are spending money. Your electric bill is getting larger, your rent or mortgage is coming due, and your body is burning calories that have to be replaced with food, which costs you money. It is very difficult to escape handling finances and partaking in the financial test.

Can you think of some other ways in which you are earning or spending money right now? Do you have money in the bank? If you do it may be earning you money by gaining interest or it can also be costing you money as it is eaten up by service charges or inflation.

Finances are something all of us must deal with every day. How we deal with our finances is important. That is why *there are more than 2,000 verses in the Bible pertaining to finances.* God gives us clear biblical principles to help us learn to effectively handle our finances and to prepare us for the daily financial test we face. If you study God's Word and apply these principles, you will not only be prepared for the financial test, but you can joyfully and abundantly pass that and other tests that come your way.

As Jesus taught his disciples and the multitudes, He showed us the importance of understanding the biblical principles of finances. He often spoke of those principles. He told how God expects His followers to pay taxes, even to a corrupt government. He emphasized the importance of rightly handling our finances, so we can leave an inheritance for our family. He discussed business principles, the biblical basis for giving, and much more.

Sometimes we confuse spirituality with how much a person gives or with what a person does in church and do not realize that the true test of spirituality is conducted daily in the classroom of life. God did not confine his teachings to just the four walls of a synagogue or a church building. In both the Old and New Testament spiritual principles were extended beyond the walls of the meeting place where God's people assembled. When Jesus came He taught us that true spirituality is determined by what one does with life. Our relationship with God extends beyond our hearts and into His creation which surrounds us. The apostle Paul summed it up for us in Colossians 3:17, *"And whatsoever ye do in word or deed, do all in the name of the Lord Jesus, giving thanks to God and the Father by Him."*

All of our actions produce results. Whatever we do affects not only us but those around us, and others we do not even see. We are all accountable for what we do. The Bible says one day we will all give an account (a financial term) for what we do (1 Cor. 3:8-15). That includes an accounting for how we handle the financial test.

In Luke 16:1-13 Jesus used a parable to teach the principle that how we handle our finances is a spiritual test that determines our faithfulness to Him.

"He that is faithful in that which is least (financial matters) *is faithful also in much* (other spiritual matters)...*If therefore ye have not been faithful in the unrighteous mammon* (finances), *who will commit to your trust the true riches"* (Luke 16:10-11).

How you do on the financial test is a spiritual matter with far-reaching consequences.

Why Do We Have Such a Hard Time with the Test?

If the Bible has so much to say about finances, why do we have such a hard time dealing with the daily financial test we face?

One reason is that many of us were never taught the biblical principles of finances. After teaching on the biblical principles of finances, I have heard accountants, attorneys, and doctors all comment that they have never heard such things taught before, though they can see that the principles are clearly taught in the Bible.

In his epistle to the Romans, Paul said "How shall they believe in Him of whom they have not heard?" The same can be said regarding the biblical principles of finances. How can people apply that which they have not heard?

Many have been taught what the Bible says about giving, but that is such a small part of what the Bible says about finances. There must be more teaching on *all* of the biblical principles of finances, not just on giving.

The biblical principles of finances related to daily living have been neglected too long and Christians and churches are suffering because of it. People must be taught the principles so they can pass the test and gain the victory in the area of finances. The question is not who should have taught you these principles, the question now is what will you do with these principles once you learn them, and will you teach them to others (2 Tim. 2:2)?

Another reason the financial test is so hard is because in the midst of the test, we often lose sight of God as our provider and put our eyes on the money itself. Instead of using the finances as a means to serve God we find ourselves serving money. Finances capture our hearts.

Paul warned us in 1 Timothy 6:10, "For the love of money is the root of all evil: which while some coveted after, they have erred from the faith, and pierced themselves through with many sorrows."

When Jesus taught about the financial test in Luke 16, He closed His teaching with a warning to which we all must carefully listen, "No man can serve two masters: for either he will hate the one, and love the other; or else he will hold to the one and despise the other. Ye cannot serve God and mammon (money)."

Most of us would say we don't *serve* money, but without realizing it we often do. In fact, one of our greatest problems is that we have been deluded into thinking we "need" money. That thinking traps us into serving money instead of God. That thinking often causes us anxiety when the bills seem larger than our resources. That thinking makes us think we earn what we have ourselves and blinds us to the one who desires to give us all things (Rom. 8:32). That thinking causes us to put our jobs before God, to put profitability before righteousness, to compromise, and to make wrong choices we live to regret later.

You may be thinking, but how can I survive if I don't have money? Let me ask you this question, Why do you need money? Why not take a moment and make a list of the things you need money for?

What items are on your list? Perhaps you listed items to maintain your well being, like food and clothing. In Matthew 6:25-34 Jesus told us, it is He who provides those things for us, it is not our income-earning capabilities.

Was the provision of shelter and security on your list? The first and the twenty-third Psalms tell us that God is our source and shelter, not our methods, our efforts or our money.

Was financing God's work on your list? Psalm 50:10 tells us He owns the cattle on a thousand hills. God does not *need* our money to carry out His work. He just allows us to give to His work, for our benefit, for our blessing. It is all part of the test.

Money is only a useful tool to help us secure the things we need, but we must always remember it is only a tool, an instrument in the test of our faithfulness. God alone is our source, not money. Too often money deceives us into thinking we must have it. It takes our eyes away from the true source, the one who is greater than money, the one who is life Himself (John 14:6).

When we learn to get our eyes off of money and onto God, we can learn what He says about money and can learn to use the tool He has entrusted to us to pass the test.

Those Who Failed the Financial Test

Throughout the Bible we are introduced to many people who took the financial test. Some passed but many failed. Each of these were included in the Bible so we could learn from their lives (2 Tim. 3:16-17; 1 Cor. 10:6; 11:1).

The Rich Man Who Hoarded
(Luke 12:13-21)

One man had a problem with his brother. The brother would not divide his inheritance with him. The man came to Jesus and heard a parable about a rich man who failed the financial test. Apparently the man in the parable was much like the man who was having the problem with his brother (Luke 12:13-21). In His teaching, Jesus did not condemn the rich man for being rich. Money is not evil in itself, nor is it wrong to be rich. Money is only a tool. When we fall in love with the tool or use it incorrectly, a problem arises. The rich man received an abundance but did not glorify God with it, nor acknowledge God as his source. Notice in Scripture all the personal pronouns the rich man uses as he speaks to himself. He depended on his own efforts and his abundance instead of God. He hoarded it as a means of future provision, without acknowledging God as his source and, therefore, failed the test. There is nothing wrong with providing for the future. In fact God expects us to provide for the future, but it was the rich man's godless, self-centered attitude which God condemned.

The Rich Young Ruler
(Luke 18:18-27)

Another time, a rich young ruler approached Jesus and asked what he could do to inherit eternal life (Luke 18:18-27). Jesus made it clear that there is nothing one can *do* to inherit eternal life. Jesus mentioned the fifth through the ninth commandments to the rich young ruler. The young man said he had kept all of them. He was a good man. Jesus then put him to the ultimate test. He asked the young man for the thing which was most dear to him, his money, to see if he was willing to put his desire for eternal life first. It was a difficult test and the man failed. He put his money before God. It is not necessary to sell everything we have to follow God, but we must be willing to do that which God desires.

The Prodigal Son
(Luke 15:11-24)

There is another person we can learn from – one who failed the financial test but learned from his failure. This person is found in one of the most well-known parables Jesus ever told, the story of the Prodigal Son (Luke 15:11-24). A wealthy father had a son who did not learn to be grateful for the things he possessed. He had an *"I deserve"* attitude. He also wanted instant gratification without working for the things he sought to enjoy. He asked his father to give him his inheritance while he was living. When his father gave it to him, the prodigal son went off to the city and sought pleasure from his money instead of God. He wasted what he had and failed the financial test. It was not till after he lost it all and hit bottom that he repented and went home. He learned that forgiveness awaits those who humble themselves, acknowledge their failures, and return to the place of blessing.

Achan
(Josh. 6:17-18; 7:11, 20-21)

There was also Achan, the one who wanted something so bad he was willing to violate God's command to get it (Josh.

6:17-18; 7:11, 20-21). When the children of Israel won their miraculous victory at Jericho, God told them not to keep any of the spoils from the battle. When Achan entered the city he saw the treasures of Jericho and coveted what was not his. He violated God's Word, took what he was not supposed to take, and hid it in his tent. He failed the test. If he had only waited for God's timing, he would have had even more than what he took. God wanted to be honored with the firstfruits of the land. In the victories that followed Jericho, God allowed the people to keep the spoils.

Others Who Failed Their Financial Test
(2 Chron. 28:21; Luke 19:11-17; Judg. 16:5)

King Ahaz used God's money to get out of a jam (2 Chron. 28:21). The unfaithful servant did not invest what was given him (Luke 19:11-17). Delilah traded love for money (Judg. 16:5). All of these people failed the test.

Those Who Passed the Financial Test

Though many failed the financial test, there were some who passed it with flying colors.

Abraham's Four Financial Tests

Abraham came from a very close family. At 75 years old, he and his wife, Sarai, who was 65, lived in Haran with his father and other relatives (Gen. 11:26-32). Abraham underwent four financial tests.

The first test was to see if he was willing to leave his home and family and trust God to direct and provide for him (Gen. 12:1-3). He was settled in Haran and had prospered there, but God told him to leave without knowing where he was going. There was a promise of blessing but not of a home or income. It would take total trust to leave and follow God. Abraham passed that test (Gen. 12:4-7). He left his father and home trusting God with his life, his future, his family, and his provisions. He even took along his nephew, Lot, whose father had passed away, so he too could share in the blessings to come.

Abraham didn't do as well on his second test. God wanted to see if Abraham would trust Him and stay in the place God lead him, even in difficult times (Gen. 12:10). God led Abraham to an area east of Bethel and famine hit the land. He did not stay and trust God to provide. He failed the test. Abraham took things into his own hands and went to Egypt where he shouldn't have gone. He sought from the world what God would have provided for him had he stayed in the place of blessing.

On his third test Abraham improved. The third test was to see if Abraham would help his family, even if it meant personal loss (Gen. 13:1-8). A conflict had arisen between Abraham's workers and those of his nephew Lot. Would Abraham, the uncle, the one to whom the land was promised, tell Lot to leave? If he were to give Lot some land, would he first choose the best for himself and then give Lot that which was left? Abraham passed this test.

Soon Abraham had another financial test. His nephew Lot and the people of Sodom were carried away in battle. Abraham and his men came to their rescue. As the victor in the battle Abraham was entitled to the people and to the possessions he had rescued (Gen. 14:13-19). Would he claim the spoils of battle, which were rightly due him? What place would God play in his life when the man of God comes to greet him after the victory? On this fourth test Abraham did exceptionally well. As he met God's man he honored God and gave him tithes of everything. He then refused to keep that which was rightly his so that God would get all the glory for being the one who made him prosperous (Gen. 14:20-24).

Joseph's Three Financial Tests

Another man who was victorious in the test was Joseph. Like Abraham he too faced a series of financial tests. Joseph was the son of Jacob and a great-grandson of Abraham. He had 11 brothers and grew up in a prosperous family. He was his father's favorite son, and the favoritism his father showed toward him caused strained relations between him and his brothers. One day some of his brothers plotted to kill him, but instead sold him into slavery. He lost everything but his life (Gen. 36:7; 37:1-36).

Joseph's first test came as a slave in Egypt (Gen. 37:23-26). In Egypt, as a servant to Potiphar, he prospered by applying biblical principles to his life. This raised him to the position of business administrator of Potiphar's financial affairs. In the midst of this prosperity came the test. Potiphar's wife wanted Joseph to get sexually involved with her. Would he violate a clear directive of Scripture to keep what he had gained?

Joseph passed the test (Gen. 39:7-15). He was willing to lose all he had gained in order to remain faithful to his God and to his employer. He would not compromise morality for financial gain or for his own comfort.

His second test came when he was faced with an opportunity to apply a difficult solution. God gave Pharaoh a dream showing him there would be seven years of prosperity followed by seven years of terrible famine. Pharaoh did not understand the dream. God gave Joseph the interpretation of the dream. Pharaoh set Joseph up as second in command over the economy of Egypt. What would he do in the times of prosperity, how would he handle the test, knowing hard times were coming (Gen. 41:1-46)?

Joseph passed this test too. In the times of prosperity Joseph laid aside food and seed for the coming hard times. No one else in the land did this; no one else prepared (Gen. 41:47-57; 47:13-25). When hard times came, even when the money system failed (Gen. 47:15), Joseph had secured stability for both his family and his master.

Perhaps the hardest test Joseph faced was the last. The famine had reached as far as Canaan where Joseph's father and brothers lived. They came to Egypt for help. The test came when the brothers who had sold him into slavery stood before him for help. Would he help them or send them away, now that the tables were turned and the power was in his hands? Joseph could have dealt harshly with his brothers who dealt so harshly with him in the past. What would he do? He did leave them wondering for a while, but he passed the test and forgave them. He assumed the responsibility which he had the capabilities of fulfilling. He was able to do it because he had faithfully adhered to God's principles of finances.

Others Who Passed Their Financial Test

Job remained faithful to God, even when all of his possessions were taken away (Job 1:12-19; 2:7-9; 4:1f.). Solomon, who when given the opportunity to ask for anything in the world, asked for God's wisdom instead of finances (1 Kings 3:3-10). Barnabas, who when he saw the need among his fellow believers, sold some of his possessions to help meet the need (Acts 4:32-37).

Many of these people probably did not realize they were taking the financial test, but each of them passed their test and saw God's abundant blessings in their lives as a result. How are you doing on your test?

For Review and Reflection...

1. Why do we have such a hard time with the financial test?

2. What can you learn from those who failed their test?

3. What can you learn from those who passed their test?

4. What financial test are you facing now?

Chapter Two
WHAT IS GOD'S STANDARD FOR YOUR LIFE?

God Wants You to Experience Fullness of Joy

There are millions and millions of people who go through life without ever knowing the wonderful things God has in store for them. Many never experience the gift of eternal life and the joy salvation can bring. There are also many Christians who have never experienced the fulness of joy or victory God desires them to have.

The words *Christian* and *life* are intimately connected. To be a Christian is to have life. That life is much more than adhering to a system of beliefs and is certainly more than just receiving salvation. Salvation is not the termination point which one strives to attain, but the commencement point from which the whole Christian life begins. God does not give us salvation, then leave us alone to wait for His return so one day we can experience the joys of eternal life. He wants us to experience that joy now. You don't have to wait until you die to experience the joys of eternal life. If you will learn to walk in obedience to God's principles and learn what His standard for your life is, then you can experience His joy right now.

The Christian has a new life which is different from the world. That new life has a new meaning, a new purpose, and new standards which produce a different lifestyle. We must present all that we have to God and transform the way we look at life, to truly appreciate that new standard of life and to know the abundance of joy which comes from living according to God's will (Rom. 12:1-2).

This is especially true in the area of personal finances. Many people do not understand God's standard for their lives or the principles in His Word by which He wants us to live. To miss that is to miss out on the tremendous blessings God wants you to experience.

God Wants His Children to Prosper

Numerous times in the Bible, God says He wants His children to prosper (Psalm 1:3; Josh. 1:7-8; 2 Cor. 9:8). In a number of instances that prosperity refers to both physical and spiritual prosperity. But the greatest emphasis in God's Word is placed on spiritual prosperity.

Joseph was a good example of someone who prospered both spiritually and physically. He faithfully applied God's principles to his life, even as a prisoner in Egypt (Gen.39:2-3, 23). The Lord made him prosper and others recognized that.

It is important however, to remember that financial prosperity by itself is not a sign of spirituality. Many who are financially prosperous never come to know salvation. Jesus explained this as He dealt with the rich young ruler (Matt. 19:16-26). The young man loved his riches too much to turn to God. Often those who are rich either trust their riches or their own abilities and won't humble themselves before God.

The believers which the apostle James addressed in his epistle, confused financial prosperity with spirituality. It caused them to neglect the people to whom they needed to minister (James 2:1-9).

Someone can be financially prosperous, in the worldly sense of the word, without being spiritually prosperous. They may have temporary pleasure and happiness, but they cannot have the true lasting joy and fulfillment they seek, without Christ. Financial prosperity without spiritual prosperity is truly empty (Eccl. 2:1-11).

It is encouraging to know that the prosperity God has for His children comes without the emptiness that comes with the prosperity the world offers (Prov. 10:22). The true prosperity God has for us comes from applying God's principles (Deut. 29:9; Josh. 1:7-8). That prosperity is different than the world's idea of prosperity. Sometimes it can mean an abundance of this world's goods but most of the time it means the prosperity of having our needs met and *some* of our wants and desires (Ps. 37:4; Matt.

7:7-11). Ultimately the prosperity God wants us to have will provide us goods and riches which are set aside for eternity, ones that no person can take away from us (Matt. 6:19-21).

Our goal should not be prosperity, but to please God (Luke 12:31-32; Matt. 6:33). If we desire to please God, He can add to our lives the things that will reflect His glory so others can see His greatness and goodness to and through us and come to know Him too. For us to experience that we must understand the principle of stewardship.

Understanding the Principle of Stewardship

Imagine what it would be like if a king invited you to come to live in one of his palaces and gave you the freedom to use everything there, if you would only acknowledge his ownership and use his estate carefully. You would not own anything but would have full use of it for all your life and for the life of your children, grandchildren, and any other descendant of yours who chooses to accept the offer. You would have all the benefits of ownership, without actually owning anything. Even though you would not own anything, you would be prosperous.

That is what God offers you. God, the king of creation, the one who created this world and rightly holds the title to all that is within it, wants to share His riches with you (Gen. 1:1; Ps. 24:1; Rom. 8:32). As a child of the King, you become heirs with God and joint-heirs with Christ (Rom. 8:15-17). You will share in the riches of glory one day, but sharing in His riches is not just a tomorrow proposition, it can be a present reality. The King has entrusted some of His riches to you now and wants to entrust more to you, but you must understand the principle of stewardship and be faithful to it to fully experience what He has for you now.

God Owns Everything

The first aspect of stewardship which must be understood is that *God is the owner*. God created us and everything else (Gen. 1:1, 27; Ps. 139:14). Everything in this world was either made by

God or assembled by man from things God made (John 1:3). Since everything in this world was made by Him, everything – including us – belongs to Him (Ps. 24:1). He is both Creator and Owner.

The most valuable thing we can have in this world is our salvation. It is not something we can earn ourselves; it comes as a gift, from God, to us. All we need to do to receive it, is to believe and accept it in faith (Eph. 2:8-9). That one gift alone makes us the most prosperous people on this earth, regardless of our financial condition (2 Pet. 1:3-4). Have you received the wonderful gift of salvation?

One of the biblical words that describes salvation is the word *redemption* (Rom. 3:24; Heb. 9:11-12). It means we have been *bought back*. God is the only one who can buy us back from the penalty and punishment of sin, which we all deserve (Rom. 3:23; Because God redeemed us, He owns us and wants us to serve Him (1 Cor. 6:19-20; Rom. 6:18). We no longer have to serve sin and a world which passes away. We can serve Him, who is eternal, who gives us life, righteousness and every good thing (Rom. 6:18; James 1:17). Serving Him truly makes us prosperous.

One of our biggest problems comes when we get the idea that what we have belongs to us. Many people live their lives with this false belief. They have the *this much is God's* and *this much is mine* attitude. It is so important for us to understand that God owns us and all we have.

Many people do not want anyone else telling them what to do with their finances. They view finances as something which is very personal. They have fallen prey to the lie of Satan, who wants them to remain in the dark about God's principles of finances. He does not want them to experience God's blessing. They seek to handle things their own way. That sets them up for a lot of frustration and eventually for a fall. It leaves them away from the abundant blessings God has for them.

When we accept God's ownership of us and all we have, then we can place the care and trust of all we have in His hands and simply use it, under His direction, for His glory. Have you acknowledged God's ownership of all you have? Are you willing to allow Him to direct you in order to use it most effectively for Him?

We Are Stewards of All God Has Entrusted to Us

Not only does God own us, but He also owns everything else in this world. All that we have is entrusted to us by God. He is like the king who allows us to live in His castle. He wants to freely give us the use of that which He owns. He just asks us to be *faithful stewards* of that which He has entrusted to us (1 Cor. 4:1-2).

A steward, in the biblical sense of the word, is basically a manager. God has entrusted His riches to us, so we may manage them for Him. That is both a great blessing and a great responsibility.

That stewardship extends to the way we use our time, our talents, and our treasure. The purpose of this book is to help identify the biblical principles of finances, so you can apply them to your life and properly manage that which God has entrusted to you, so you can be a faithful steward.

One exciting aspect of stewardship is that God gives us the full use and benefit of the things He has entrusted to us. All He asks is that we faithfully apply His principles in our life (1 Cor. 4:2; Josh. 1:8). To faithfully apply His principles, we must learn what they are.

In Luke's Gospel we learn that *if we want to be a faithful steward we need God's wisdom* (Luke 12:42-47). He wants us to use His estate carefully. The decisions we make which create financial hardships and put a strain on God's estate, are those made without God's wisdom.

Our own pride is often our greatest stumbling block (Prov. 16:18; 1 Cor. 10:12). Often we think we know the best way to do things, but God says we need His help to manage His estate. The wonderful thing is, He will help us if we ask Him. The wisdom we need can be ours with prayer and Bible study. James 1:5 says we can ask God for His wisdom and He will give it to us.

In Proverbs, God tells us that one reason He gave us that book was to help us get a handle on His wisdom (Prov. 1:2). Proverbs says wisdom calls out to us, but we must look for it if we want it (Prov. 1:20; 2:1-6). We can have God's wisdom to be the kind of stewards we should be.

Have you asked God for His wisdom to help you be a good steward? Will you seek out and apply the principles from God's Word to make you become a good steward?

We Must Give an Account of Our Stewardship

As stewards of all God has entrusted to us, we will one day give an *account* for how we handle His estate (2 Cor. 5:10). The word *account* is a financial term. It implies records are being kept. A full accounting is being made of how we transact God's business.

Some people look at this responsibility with fear, rather than joy. Some are afraid to do anything with what God has given them, for fear they may make a mistake and be punished. God is not looking to punish you, He wants to reward you.

Some people do not apply His principles because they are too lazy to apply the diligence required. They seek the easy way out. In Luke 19:11-27, Jesus uses a parable to explain the principle of faithfulness and stewardship and to deal with these attitudes.

In the parable we find a nobleman who calls ten of his servants together and commits a portion of his estate to their trust. He gives them each one pound (*mina*) to use wisely.

One pound was the equivalent of 100 *denarii*. A denarius was a day's wage for a working man. Therefore, this nobleman entrusted to each servant the equivalent of more than four months wages all at once. How much money would that be for you? That certainly is not an insignificant amount of money.

What would you do if someone gave you that much money and said go use this wisely?

When the nobleman returned, each of the servants were brought before him to give an account of how they used their portion of their master's estate. The passage tells us what happened with three of the servants.

The first one multiplied what he was given, ten times. The master congratulated him and rewarded him by putting him in charge of ten cities.

The second one multiplied what he was given, five times. He too was congratulated and rewarded proportionately by being put in charge of five cities.

The third came back with the same amount he was given. He misunderstood his master and feared him, so he did not use what he was given. Instead he hid the pound, then brought back the same amount. The master called him a wicked servant. He told the servant he should have at least given the money to a bank to earn some interest on it. There was no reward for the third servant, for there was no faithful service.

There are many lessons which can be learned from this parable. In the context of stewardship and the biblical principles of finances, we see that God entrusts his riches to us for us to use wisely for Him. He expects us to use that which He has given us in a way that multiplies it. He does not want what He gives us to sit idle.

We also see that **rewards are given according to our faithfulness.** Are you using wisely what God has given you? Are you seeking to multiply it for His glory?

God's Word makes it clear that God wants to bless us (Eph. 1:3; 1 Peter 3:9; Ps. 103:2). Those blessings are in proportion to our faithfulness and our obedience to Him (Prov. 8:32; 10:6; 28:20).

The blessings God gives are better and more enduring than the temporary pleasure this world can offer (Heb. 11:25; 2 Cor.

4:17-18). His blessings are eternal. They won't rust away or wear out like a lot of the things we have and think are important (Matt. 6:20; 25:21).

His blessings are also spiritual. These things can never be bought. The joy unspeakable, the peace that passes all understanding, and the love that never fails (1 Peter 1:8; Phil 4:7; 1 Cor 13:8). Those who possess such blessings are truly prosperous.

Besides giving us eternal and spiritual blessings, God also gives us physical blessings. He blesses us in ways that help us to enjoy the world in which we live. As good stewards we must learn to see those blessings and thank Him for them. They may not always be what we want, but they will always be what we need and what is best for us.

Understanding the Principle of Contentment

The next basic biblical principle of finances we must understand is that of contentment – one of the hardest principles. If we learn and apply this one, in God's way, we will find a tremendous handle on life, which will produce a real stability for us in uncertain times.

Many people are not content with what they have. They are always seeking more than they have and often get caught up in the never-ending spiral of trying to accumulate more and more. In the process they often lose sight of what God has for them.

Some people, on the other hand, are content with less than they should have and have lost sight of what God has for them.

What does God want us to be content with? What is the standard by which He wants believers to live?

Understanding the Difference Between Needs And Wants

First, it is important to learn the distinction between *needs* and *wants*. We often say we *need* something, when in reality, it is not something we *need*, but something we *want*.

For example, you *need* food. Everyone of us needs food to carry on the existence God has for us on this earth. If you do not eat you will eventually die. When you feel the pangs of hunger or smell the fresh aroma of a steak cooking on the grill, you may feel you need to have a steak. In reality, you *want* a steak, but you do not *need* a steak, what you need is food. Steak does happen to be food and there is nothing wrong with wanting a steak. But it is important to learn to distinguish between a need and a want. God has promised to meet all our needs, but he has not said he will give us all our wants.

Consider the need for shelter. Everyone needs some place to put their head down at night. Many people feel they need to own a home. There is nothing wrong with owning a home, if it is done in God's way, but you do not *need* to own a home. You may *want* to own a home, but you do not *need* to own a home. Jesus and many of His followers never owned a home.

God has promised to meet all our needs. *"But my God shall supply all your need according to His riches in glory by Christ Jesus"* (Phil. 4:19).

Many of our problems come when we fail to make the proper distinction between what we need and what we want.

One problem is that people *want* more than they *need*. The Bible calls that **covetousness**. It is a very serious problem, so serious that God warned us against it in the Ten Commandments (Exod. 20:17).

Another problem is when people feel they *deserve* more than they have. That problem is called **unthankfulness** and is one of the first steps on the downward spiral of sin mentioned in Romans 1:21-32.

Others have a problem distinguishing between needs and wants and put themselves before God. They suffer from the problem known as **selfishness**. They want what they want for themselves and will disregard God's principles to get it.

Covetousness, unthankfulness, and selfishness are common problems, even in the Christian community. Sometimes the root cause is a desire to want more for the family, but people get caught in the snare of the Devil (1 Tim. 6:8-9; 2 Tim. 2:26). That is why it is so important to understand the principles of stewardship and contentment.

The principle of contentment is not one we naturally accept. We all are born with a sin nature and naturally desire more than we need (Rom. 3:10-12; James 1:14-15; 4:2). The monetary system of this world seeks to draw even the believer away from God to serve it (Matt. 6:19-24).

Too many people are not content with what they have. They believe they deserve more and are unthankful for what God has given them. Have you ever felt like that? Have you ever said, "God I deserve better than this."

We should be so thankful we don't get what we deserve. If we got what we truly deserved, we'd be spending eternity apart from God right now, being punished for our sins. Only the grace of God saves us and the mercy of God keeps us from suffering the punishment of sin.

"For he hath made Him to be sin for us, who knew no sin; that we might be made the righteousness of God in Him" (2 Cor. 5:21).

How ironic that we deserve to be punished for our sins and He who never sinned, died to give us life. How can we still cry out "give me what I deserve." How foolish we are sometimes.

What Should We Be Content With?

If we acknowledge that God does want us to be content, what does He expect us to be content with?

The Bible tells us *we are to learn to be content in whatever situation we are in* (Phil. 4:11). That is not always easy, especially if you are experiencing hard times. If the bills are rising over your head and everything is falling apart around about you, how can you be content?

Remember 1 Timothy 6:6, *"But godliness with contentment is great gain."* Contentment is not based on circumstances but on the goodness of God. You need to realize you are in your current situation for one of two reasons: either you violated a biblical principle and are suffering some of the consequences or God is using you to show His grace and glory.

You must ask yourself, is there any known sin in my life which I have not confessed or any biblical principle I know I should have applied but did not? Remember, Psalm 66:18, *"If I regard iniquity in my heart, the Lord will not hear me."* Confess that sin to God and experience His cleansing. *"If we confess our sins, He is faithful and just to forgive us our sins, and to cleanse us from all unrighteousness"* (1 John 1:9).

Sometimes you cannot see any particular principle you may have violated, but your situation is still difficult. God wants you to be content. You need to accept what God is doing in your life and be content with your current situation, until He leads you out of it or changes it.

He did not say only be content under pleasant circumstances. God brought Joseph to Egypt as a prisoner under unpleasant circumstance, but He did it to bless him and generations to come (Gen. 39-50).

No matter how bleak your picture seems, you need to acknowledge God, thank Him, and accept His will for your life.

Another thing we are to be content with is *our wages* (Luke 3:14). Jesus spoke those words to a group of underpaid soldiers.

It seems everyone wants to be paid more for what they do. Every year people look for a pay raise because of rising costs. When they get their raise, the costs of goods and services go up and they never get ahead. People are earning more today than ever before, but their buying power is declining. It is an endless cycle.

One reason we want higher wages is because we make the mistake of thinking that money meets our needs. But money doesn't meet our needs, God does. Money is only a tool God uses. We must be content with our wages.

The Two Things God Promised Us

There are really only two material things God has promised for us. If we can learn to be content with just those two things, we would experience the real blessing of contentment and be on our way to financial freedom. Those two things are **food and clothing.**

"Having food and raiment (clothing) *let us therewith be content"* (1 Tim. 6:8).

Food and clothing, the two areas we seem to cut back on when the finances are tight, are the two things God promised to provide. Fathers, it seems strange that we, who share one of God's titles, "Father," should do God and our families such a disservice by cutting back on the two very things He promised.

Sometimes we overdo it in those two areas and can stand to cut back. The key is learning to distinguish between *needs* and *wants.* Remember the steak illustration. We should have sufficient food to feed us and enough clothing to cloth us. It would be very good if we could learn to be content with that standard, because that is what God has promised to provide for us.

Pray for Your Daily Bread

Even though God has promised to provide food and clothing and wants us to be content with that, He told us we still need to pray daily for those items (Matt. 6:11, 25-34). Even though you may have a job or another source of income, remember to pray for your daily bread, the daily needs which God wants to meet in our lives. Many, many people go into debt because of failure to heed this simple command from our Lord.

Remember, God is our source. He is the one who provides our needs. Oh, yes, you may work for the income to provide those items, but He gives you the strength, ability, and job to do that.

"But godliness with contentment is great gain," 1 Timothy 6:6. If you will learn to apply the principle of contentment to

your life and couple it with obedience to the principles you learn from His Word, you will find it very profitable.

Remember you are a steward of what God entrusts to you. Acknowledge His ownership of you and all you have. Be thankful for what He has given you and the situations He allows you to be in. Learn to distinguish between what you *need* and what you *want* and be content as He meets your needs. If you apply these principles to your life you are ready to experience the joy of applying God's order of finances to your life.

For Review and Reflection . . .

1. In what way does God want you to prosper?

2. How does that differ from the way the world prospers?

3. What does it mean to be a steward for God?

4. How can you be a better steward?

5. What does God mean when He says He wants you to be content?

Chapter Three
UNDERSTANDING GOD'S ORDER IN FINANCES

We Need to Apply God's Principles in His Order

I like chocolate chip cookies, especially the ones with lots of chocolate chips in them. I even like chocolate chips by themselves. But I do not like flour or baking soda. Have you ever tasted them by themselves? I personally don't think they taste good alone. And what about vanilla? It smells good but it sure does taste awful. The interesting thing is, if you mix those ingredients with some brown sugar, eggs, and a lot of chocolate chips, carefully following the recipe, then apply heat to the mixture, it will produce delicious chocolate chip cookies.

What would happen if you left out the bitter tasting ingredients from the recipe? What would happen if you beat the mixture too long or applied the heat at the wrong time? Your delicious chocolate chip cookies would not turn out right.

The same is true with God's principles. God's principles cannot be taken piece meal. They are like the ingredients in the recipe. Taken by themselves, you may find some of the individual principles hard to swallow and may wonder why they are there. But if you follow His recipe, applying each principle in the order He has designed, you will find a pleasing product in the end.

As God provides us with funds, we are to allocate them according to His order, following His recipe, applying His principles. It is true that we will receive His blessing for following His principles and observing His order in our finances, but our motivation should not be to get a blessing. Our obedience should be an expression of love for the One who freely gave us all things (Matt. 10:8; Rom. 8:32).

When all income is received, we should allocate it in the following order, based on the financial priorities and responsibilities with which God has entrusted us.

Tithe or Firstfruits
(Prov. 3:1-12; Mal. 3:7-12)

God expects us to acknowledge His ownership of all we have by putting Him first. That applies to every area of our lives, including the area of finances.

There were different types of giving in the Bible. If you were to conduct a study of the various biblical methods of giving, you would find that they include the giving of tithes, alms, and offerings. The most basic type of giving, which transcends both testaments, is firstfruits, also known as the tithe.

A Look at What the Bible Says about Tithe or Firstfruits

The word *tithe* means ten percent. Under the Old Testament Law, God's people were required to bring three tithes to God's house. One was used to maintain the ministry (Num. 18:12-14, 21). One was used to support the priests and other people in the ministry and to carry out a benevolent ministry (Deut. 14:22f.). The third tithe was brought every three years, to provide an inheritance for the priests and their families, because they were not given land or other means of producing income to provide for their families.

This meant tithing for each person averaged 23.33 percent a year. This money, from the tithes, was distributed as follows:

43% – Supported the Priests

29% – Was for Local Ministry

14% – Was used for Special Outreach to People

14% – Was used for a Retirement Fund and Inheritance (for the priests and their families)

Alms are mentioned in the Gospels and in the Acts of the Apostles (Luke 12:33; Acts 3:2-3). They generally entailed giving 20 percent of one's income for the poor. Many Muslims still follow this practice.

The *offering* was an amount given for a specific purpose. Often it was for the construction or repair of buildings (Exod.

30:11-16). The offering was generally freewill and was given in proportion to God's blessing, as one was able to give (Deut. 16:16-17).

The giving of the tithe *pre-dates* the giving of the law. Abraham gave the tithe before the law was given (Gen. 14:20). In Hebrews 7:1-10, we are told to follow Abraham's example.

The giving of the tithe *post-dates* the law. Malachi 3:7-12 tells us to give the tithe. It says that the tithe allows God to show Himself as God on our behalf, through physical blessings.

The giving of the tithe also *transcends* the law. Jesus said He came to fulfill the law and the prophets, the two major sections in the Old Testament (Matt. 5:17). Those sections are given for our example, but the New Testament believer is not bound by the precepts and laws in them (Eph. 2:14-15). But there is a third section found in the Old Testament, which is still applicable for the New Testament believer. It is the psalms section of the Bible and is comprised of the books of Job, Psalms, Proverbs, Ecclesiastes, and Song of Solomon (Eph. 5:18; Col. 3:16).

Proverbs 3:1-12 gives an extensive teaching on the firstfruits principle, the first tithe. This is as applicable today as it was in the Old Testament and will remain so in the future. Let us take a brief look at this passage.

"My son, forget not my law; but let thine heart keep my commandments" (verse 1). God says He wants obedience in this matter.

"For length of days, and long life, and peace, shall they add to thee" (verse 2). God promises blessing for obedience in this matter.

"Let not mercy and truth forsake thee: bind them about they neck; write them upon the table of thine heart" (verse 3). God warns us not to forget His mercy toward us, nor the truth of this teaching, but exhorts us to internalize (memorize and apply) this principle.

"So shalt thou find favour and good understanding in the

sight of God and man" (verse 4). Applying this principle will affect our relationship with God and Man.

"Trust in the Lord with all thine heart; and lean not unto thine own understanding" (verse 5). Our reasoning will tell us not to apply this principle. We must trust God and do it.

"In all thy ways acknowledge Him, and He shall direct thy paths" (verse 6). God will put His clear direction in our lives if we will apply this principle.

"Be not wise in thine own eyes: fear the Lord, and depart from evil" (verse 7). God gives another warning: Don't listen to our own wisdom. We will do the wrong thing. Obey this principle instead.

"It shall be health to thy navel, and marrow to thy bones" (verse 8). God gives another promise: Obedience to this principle will affect our health in a positive way.

"Honour the Lord with thy substance, and with the firstfruits of all thine increase" (verse 9). After getting our attention God now gives us the principle: Honor God by giving Him the Firstfruits (the first tithe) of all your increase (income).

"So shall thy barns be filled with plenty, and thy presses shall burst out with new wine" (verse 10). God gives another promise: He will meet our needs and even give us more (v.10).

"My son, despise not the chastening of the Lord; neither be weary of His correction: For whom the Lord loveth He correcteth; even as a father the son in whom he delighteth" (verses 11-12). God gives another warning: He loves us so much He will discipline us, no matter how long it takes, if we do not apply the firstfruits principle (v.11-12).

How to Apply the Biblical Teaching on Tithe or Firstfruits

First, figure the first 10 percent of all your gross income. If you put the tithe (firstfruits) after taxes or expenses, then God is not being put first. This area comes before taxes, family needs, and debt repayment.

Giving God the tithe acknowledges His ownership in your life and allows Him to work miraculously in His provision for you (Mal. 3:7-12). The firstfruits should be given through the local church (1 Cor. 16:1-2).

Taxes
(Matt. 22:15-22; Rom. 13:1-7)

This is the next area of financial responsibility. If you are an employee you usually do not have a choice in dealing with this area of financial responsibility. The government takes its share of your income before you do. The amount you must give is determined by the government, though certain exemptions allow you to reduce the amount you must give.

A Look at What the Bible Says about Taxes

We Must Pay Our Taxes. Jesus taught us to *"render unto Caesar what is Caesars and unto God what is God's"* (Matt. 22:21). He was telling his followers they were expected to pay their taxes, even to the corrupt Roman government.

Paul also reinforced this teaching in his epistle to the Romans. *"For this cause pay ye tribute also..."* (Rom. 13:6). The word tribute refers to taxes. The believer is expected to pay his taxes.

We Must Be Honest. As we pay our taxes we are to be honest (Rom. 12:17). Cheating on our taxes is wrong, because it is being dishonest which is sin (2 Cor. 4:2). That also means we are to report *under the table business dealings.*

We Must Use Wisdom. We are to be wise stewards, especially in this area of paying taxes. God says *"render unto Caesar what is Caesars."* He does not say to give Caesar more than he is due. If you do not keep informed about changes in the tax law and maintain some familiarity with the tax system, you will probably pay more taxes than you should. In so doing, you are giving the government that which is God's.

How to Apply the Biblical Teaching on Taxes

Pay Your Taxes On Time. Be sure to pay your taxes on time. Employees usually have no choice, it is automatically deducted for you. Self-employed people must deduct their own taxes and may have to file quarterly estimated tax returns.

Keep Accurate Records. Keep accurate records, they will help you fill out your taxes properly. If you do not know how to handle this area of your finances, you may be able to learn how. If you have tried and it overwhelms you, you may want to work with an accountant or professional tax-preparer. Remember, not all tax preparers will do your taxes properly. Many will not be familiar with the biblical principles you follow or the tax laws which work to your advantage.

Learn How to Reduce Your Tax Burden. If you pay a lot of taxes, learn about tax shelters and tax-free investments. Those are legal ways to help reduce your tax burden.

Use all the deductions you are entitled to. If you keep getting a large tax refund, the tax laws usually allow you to increase the number of exemptions with your employer so less money is deducted from your paycheck. That can reduce the amount of your refund. Remember, when you fill out your tax returns, you must claim only the number of exemptions to which you are entitled.

If you receive a large tax refund, this is poor stewardship. It means you are giving the government more than you should when you could have earned interest on it. The government does not pay you interest on tax refunds.

Family Needs
(1 Tim. 5:8)

After the tithe and taxes are allocated, we come to a very important financial area, the area of family needs. God says the person who does not take care of this area is worse than one who denies God exists (1 Tim. 5:8).

A Look at What the Bible Says about Family Needs

God promises to provide all of your *needs* (Phil. 4:19). He will meet the needs of your family as you follow His principles (1 Tim. 5:8).

Pray for Provision. One of the most important things to remember, is God said we need to *pray* for our family needs, every day, even though He promised to provide them (Matt. 6:11).

Learn to Distinguish between Needs and Wants. Next, it is very important to learn to distinguish between *needs* and *wants*. Often we *want* more than we *need*. Sometimes funds that should be spent on *needs* are spent on *wants* and the whole balance is disturbed. Family needs must come before debt (1 Tim. 5:8; Prov. 22:26-29). Too often a debt is incurred to buy a *want* and some area of *need* suffers.

The most basic family needs which must be met are food and clothing (1 Tim. 6:8). We must learn balance in this area (Prov. 30:8-9). How much food do you really need? Do you need to eat out as often as you do?   Is that the best stewardship of God's money? How much and what type of clothing do you need? Do you really need as much as you have? Is your outward adorning the grace of the Lord which reflects from you or is it dependent on the brand name or style of clothing you wear (1 Peter 3:3-4)?

You Should Provide Shelter. Our next area of provision under family needs, is some form of *shelter*. That doesn't necessarily mean owning a house (Matt. 8:20). There are many believers around the world who do not own a house. Some rent a place, some live in tents.

The Bible does not say it is wrong to own a house. In fact, God provided land for the children of Israel so they would have a place to build their homes. Parents helped provide the land for their children to build on, then the son would establish a good form of income, get engaged, build his house, get married, and start a family. We have come far from the biblical practice and have suffered much for it. We need to get back to this practice (Prov. 24:27). This is a worthy goal for Christian parents and an admonition to those who are single.

The idea of the self-made man who can go out and do anything on his own, is contrary to the Bible picture of the spirit-filled man who depends on the Lord and the family God has given Him, and who then does great things.

You Should Budget and Save Ahead. Another principle we must consider is the concept of budgeting and saving ahead. We all face hard times, unforeseen emergencies, and items that wear out. There are some bills that come due only once or twice a year, for which we must prepare in advance.

Some Christians say believers should not have a savings account. They say God will provide each day, what we need. It is true God will provide each day what we need, but often He provides in advance.

We are exhorted to look at the ant and follow its example. The ant sets aside goods, in the prosperous time of summer, to prepare for the difficult times of winter (Prov. 6:6-11). It pictures saving ahead.

When Joseph was in Egypt, God told him to prepare in advance, during the times of plenty, for the difficult times ahead (Gen. 41).

Christians should follow this example and have some type of savings to prepare for family needs that arise. Be careful not to save too much. God does not want you to hoard (Luke 12:16-21).

The ant principle of careful stewardship and saving applies to preparing for our retirement and to leaving an inheritance for our children and grandchildren. God expects us to do both (Prov. 19:14; 2 Cor. 12:14; Prov. 13:22).

You Should Want to Provide Your Family's Wants. Besides just providing our family's needs, parents should also want to provide the *wants* for their children, as our Heavenly Father wants to give us our desires. But it must be done in concert with his principles and following his order in finances (Matt. 7:7-11).

Debts become a barrier to being able to meet the wants of

our family. One motivation for eliminating our debts should be so we will have an abundance to be able to meet our family's wants.

How to Apply the Biblical Teaching on Family Needs

Commit Your Finances to God. The first thing to do, is to pray and commit your finances to God. Then ask Him daily for the provision you need and for the wisdom to use it according to His will.

Prepare a Workable Budget. You will need some type of budget to be able to follow God's principles effectively. Drafting up a budget and trying to use one frightens many people. It is not as difficult as it seems. *The Christian Budget Bookkeeping System* has helped many families set up a workable budget and effectively apply God's principles.

The mistake most people make in trying to set up a budget is to budget their gross income for this area. You must subtract the tithe and taxes first; that provides you with a figure for your net spendable income. Figure a budget that coincides with your pay periods. It should be monthly, every two weeks or weekly, however you are paid. Self-employed people need to make a conservative estimate of their annual earnings and pay themselves a regular basic salary. That is what they should base their budget on.

Never live off the checkbook balance, live off the budget. If you are applying the ant principle, there should always be more in the checkbook than you should spend.

Determine what you should be spending on food and clothing and stick to those figures. You may have some periods of fluctuation but be careful to stick by your budget the best you can.

Budget now for long-term purchases, like a car or a new washing machine. Using the ant principle you should set aside a little each week. Your car and washer will break down, be prepared for it. You can use the interest you earn on these funds for additional debt liquidation or for wants or giving.

Set Up A Savings Plan. Set up a savings plan to prepare for hard times, the future, and your retirement.

Have Adequate Insurance. Be sure you are adequately insured, so your family is provided for in case you are no longer able to provide. Determine your insurance needs according to biblical principles and be cautious of the advice you get from insurance agents. Remember that they are salesmen and only make money if you buy their product. Don't despair when making choices regarding insurance. There are some committed Christians who are good insurance agents.

Learn to Economize. Learn to economize on your purchases and shop wisely. Wait for sales and learn how to identify good values. A lower price does not always indicate a better value.

Don't Forget Recreation. Each family *needs* some form of recreation. Be sure to budget some reasonable enjoyment in this area. You may *want* to go on a lavish vacation, but you must not cut back on your food, clothing, and shelter to do it.

Carefully Budget Your Gift-Giving. Be careful about expenditures for gifts. Birthdays, Christmas, and other events can be real budget busters. Determine who you should buy for and how much you should spend, in advance. Remember the principles of stewardship and contentment in this area.

Debt Retirement
(Rom. 13:8; Prov. 6:1-5)

After you provide the needs for your family, and before you provide their wants, you must eliminate your debts.

A Look at What the Bible Says about Debt Retirement

Beware of Borrowing. God's Word cautions strongly against borrowing. He told the children of Israel, as they were about to enter the promised land, one sign of His blessing on them would be they would not be the ones doing the borrowing, but the ones doing the lending (Deut. 28:1-15).

"And it shall come to pass, if thou shalt hearken diligently unto the voice of the Lord thy God, to observe and to do all His

commandments which I command thee this day, that the Lord thy God will set thee on high above all nations of the earth" (Deut. 28:1).

*"The Lord shall open unto thee His good treasure, the heaven to give the rain unto thy land in his season, and to bless all the work of thine hand: **and thou shalt lend unto many nations, and thou shalt not borrow"*** (Deut. 28:12).

He told them, if they did not heed His Word and apply His principles, they would be the borrower (Deut. 28:15-68).

"But it shall come to pass, if thou wilt not hearken unto the voice of the Lord thy God, to observe to do all His commandments and His statutes which I command thee this day; that all these curses shall come upon thee and overtake thee" (Deut. 28:15).

"He shall lend to thee, and thou shalt not lend to him: he shall be the head, and thou shalt be the tail" (Deut. 28:44).

Another very strong warning against going into debt is found in Paul's epistle to the Romans. *"Owe no man anything, but to love one another: for he that loveth one another hath fulfilled the law"* (Rom. 13:8).

The context deals with financial matters, such as paying taxes and paying people what they are owed. God says the best thing to do is not to be in financial debt to anyone. Instead the only debt we should have is to love others more than we do.

Beware of Guaranteeing Loans. God's Word also cautions against *surety*, which is cosigning or guaranteeing a loan for someone else (Prov. 17:18). It is interesting to note that the Hebrew word for *surety* is *arav*. Among its meanings, in modern Hebrew, is the word *mortgage*.

Pray for Your Needs. It is important to understand the principle that God expects you to pray for your needs and wants, not to take out a loan or borrow money for them, even if you have collateral to cover it (Prov. 22:26-29).

Acknowledge Your Responsibility. We must remember

that if we are in debt, it is our fault, not God's. The comforting thing to know is, if we acknowledge our fault and agree to change, He will help us. It will take obedience on our part and the diligence to apply His principles, but He will lead us out of debt.

Pay All Your Debts. Another principle to keep in mind, is that you must pay all your debts. Even though you never should have incurred them in the first place, God expects you to pay them all (Eccl. 5:4-6; Ps. 37:21).

Remember, you should not purchase your wants until you pay off your debts (Prov. 6:1-5). If you buy something you want before you pay off someone you owe money to, you are using what is rightly that other person's for your own enjoyment.

It takes diligence and concentrated effort to pay off debts. Sometimes it takes an extra job. Be sure not to violate another biblical principle if you have to work another job to pay off your debts (Prov. 6:1-5).

How to Apply the Biblical Teaching on Debt

Pray and Stop All Borrowing. Pray for your wants and needs, stop all borrowing. You must not spend more than you bring in. Draft a budget and follow it. Remember a wise man once said, "If you outgo exceeds your income, your upkeep will become your downfall."

Start Saving. Begin to save on a regular basis for items you will need or want in the future. Items will wear out and need to be replaced. Save something, even if it is only a few dollars, otherwise you will go further in debt when the actual need for the funds arrives.

Consider Selling Some Items. If you bought something on credit and are in debt, prayerfully consider selling the item to eliminate the debt.

Consider Additional Work. If tithe, taxes and family needs consume all your income, you may need to work overtime or find additional employment, until you have eliminated your debts. If you are married, it rarely works to have your wife go to work to help eliminate debt. You will usually find yourself in the trap of higher taxes and higher expenses with her working. It is not wrong for a wife to work, but it should not be to eliminate debt.

Don't Buy Wants. Be sure not to spend money on things you want until you have eliminated your debts.

If you are in debt follow the steps in the next chapter to get out of debt. When you are out of debt, the funds in this area automatically become part of your abundance and give you the ability to be involved in meeting the needs of others as well as the wants of your family.

Abundance
(2 Cor. 9:8)

God's goal is for every believer to have an abundance. Few find it because they do not apply God's principles.

A Look at What The Bible Says about Abundance

The primary reason God gives us an abundance is so we can help meet needs in other people's lives.

"And God is able to make all grace abound toward you; that ye, always having all sufficiency in all things, may abound to every good work" (2 Cor. 9:8).

Notice the many superlatives in that verse: *all, abound, always, all sufficiency, all things, abound, every good work.*

What a joy it is to help meet the needs in other people's lives. It goes beyond temporary material things, to things which are eternal (Matt. 19:21; Luke 12:13-21).

Offerings and giving to special needs and projects, as well as funds to meet our wants and desires, come mainly from this area (2 Cor. 9:6-7; Prov. 6:1-5).

When we apply God's principles there is no sorrow in riches (Prov. 10:22).

God wants to be first in this area of our lives, so glorify Him with your abundance (Col. 3:17).

How to Apply the Biblical Teaching on Abundance

Be a Good Steward. Be a good steward of everything God has entrusted to you. Take good care of what you have and learn to invest your money wisely.

Keep Some of Your Abundance Liquid. Understand the principle of liquidity. You may have some of your funds invested. Liquidity means that some of your investments should be the type that can be exchanged readily for cash, without delays. This is helpful, and sometimes necessary, to meet an immediate need.

Develop Some Written Goals. One of the best ways to prepare for an abundance, is to develop written goals that show what you would do with your abundance. We often have good intentions, but few of them are never carried out because we do not commit ourselves. It is easier to decide what you want to do with it before you have an abundance, than it is to do so when you have it in your hands. You will spend more of it on yourself than on others, if you wait until it is in your hand before you make a decision.

Develop Guidelines for Giving. You cannot give to every need presented to you. In fact, not all the appeals you receive will be ones to which you should give. Use criteria based on biblical principles to guide you in deciding where your abundance should be distributed.

There is great joy and freedom to be found in the area of abundance.

For Review and Reflection...

1. Why is it important to know and follow God's order in finances?

2. What is the firstfruits principle?

3. What are the basic family needs that should be met?

4. Why is a budget helpful?

5. What is the ant principle?

6. Why should you pay off your debts before purchasing your wants?

7. What is the main reason for having an abundance?

8. What application of God's order in finances should you make in your life now?

Chapter Four
DEBT-FREE LIVING

You Can Get Out of Debt and Stay Out of Debt

Being in debt is a frustrating, undesirable experience. Many people try repeatedly to get out of debt, but find themselves falling down the slippery slope of indebtedness over and over again. Others resign themselves to the miserable fate of being in debt for the rest of their lives and try to eke out the best existence they can. Many people just try their best to survive and accept debt as an inevitable consequence of daily existence.

One of the greatest desires many people have is to break free from the bonds of debt. They long to experience the joy of debt-free living.

There is a way out of the quagmire of debt. But to get out of debt and stay out of debt, takes an understanding and consistent application of the biblical principles of finances regarding debt and need.

Biblical Principles Regarding Debt and Need

Understanding and applying of these principles will keep you from going into debt or will help you get out of debt. They have worked for hundreds of people who have taken the time to study and apply them.

The Way We Handle Our Finances Is a Spiritual Matter
(Luke 16:10-11)

How can the way we handle our finances be a spiritual matter? Aren't spiritual matters things like praying, reading the Bible or going to church? How can a thing like finances, which causes us so many problems, be spiritual? Isn't the love of money the root of all evil?

Many misunderstandings must be cleared up. Perhaps the first one to address is, what is a spiritual matter? Somehow a false system of dualism has rooted itself in many people's minds. Under this system of dualism things are categorized as either sacred or secular. Church and related matters are considered sacred, while employment, finances and government are considered secular.

This false system of dualism is foreign to the teachings of the Bible. According to the Word of God, everything is made by God for His glory, and is sacred – even government and finances.

God is concerned about everything we are involved in and everything we do. In God's eyes, everything is spiritual. From the way we spend our day, to the job we hold, to the food we eat, and to the way we handle our finances, everything is a spiritual matter (1 Cor. 10:31; Eccl. 3:1-12; Ps. 24:1). It is important to understand that the way we handle our finances is a spiritual matter. In fact, there are more than 2,000 verses in the Bible on finances.

But isn't money an evil thing? The answer is no. Money is not evil – it is only a tool. As a tool, it can be used for either good or evil. It is not money itself, but the *love* of money which is called *the root of all evil* (1 Tim. 6:10).

In Luke 16:10-11, Jesus said: *"He that is faithful in that which is least is faithful also in much: and he that is unjust in the least is unjust also in much. If therefore ye have not been faithful in the unrighteousness mammon, who will commit to your trust the true riches."*

In the context, finances are called *that which is least*. They are called *the unrighteous mammon*. Yet God says the way we handle the *unrighteous mammon* determines how much of the *true riches* he will commit to us. Therefore, we need to study and apply God's principles in handling our finances.

God Promises to Provide Our Needs
(Phil 4:19)

Another very important principle to remember is that God

promised to meet all our needs. That promise is of utmost significance. If God has promised to supply all our needs, then we do not need to go into debt to meet them.

If you are in debt, you need to ask yourself what is wrong. Did you step out ahead of God and go into debt to purchase your *wants*? Did you misspend the funds God provided you? Do you know of any sin in your life which you have not confessed or anything God wants you to do that you have refused to do? Is God attempting to redirect you? If you are in debt, the answer to one of those questions is yes.

God Wants Us to Have Enough So We Can Give to Others
(2 Cor. 9:8)

God does not want you under the bondage of debt. He wants you to experience the joy of debt-free living. He wants you in the place of abundance.

We often want to be in the place of abundance for different reasons than God wants us there. God wants you in the place of abundance so you can be a channel for Him to flow His blessings through to others.

One reason we do not make it to the place of abundance is because often we are selfish and want things for ourselves and would not handle abundance the way God wants us to handle it. Sometimes we forget that one of the greatest joys we can experience is the joy of giving (Acts 20:35). Our selfishness often gets us into debt in the first place, and often our selfishness keeps us there.

The Bible is full of amazing paradoxes. To live, it says we must die (Gal. 2:20). To get, it says we must give (Luke 6:38): *"Give, and it shall be given unto you; good measure, pressed down, shaken together, and running over, shall men give into your bosom. For with the same measure that ye mete withal it shall be measured to you again."* God wants you and I to be a spout, through which He can pour His blessings out. Too often we get in the way and clog up the spout.

God's People Are to Lend, Not Borrow
(Deut. 28:12-44)

One of the blessings God promised His children, as they entered the promised land, was if they would follow His principles they would be lenders, not borrowers.

God wants the world to see that provision comes from Him. When God's people have financial stability, it shows the world He can provide. He then gets the glory.

I had a good Jewish friend who told me he was raised on the principle that God's people were to be lenders not borrowers. He said he applied that principle in his business and God blessed him.

He asked me why Christians, who consider themselves God's children, do not follow such a clear command?

That is a good question. God told the Jews, if they turned away from His principles, He would use a different people and provoke them to jealousy (Rom. 10:19). How can we provoke them to jealousy if we are in financial bondage? We are to be the lenders not the borrowers.

Also note that God's people were to lend to other nations, not to one another. God's people are to help meet each others' needs. We are to give or lend without interest, when a brother is in need. If we want to make money on loans, we must lend to those outside the family of God (Deut. 23:20).

When we as God's children are the lenders, rather than the borrowers, the world will be able to see that God is blessing us.

We Are Not to Be in Debt to Any Man
(Rom. 13:8; Prov. 22:26-29; Prov. 17:18)

Years ago, people used to be ashamed if they were in debt. Now going in debt seems to be the accepted thing.

God's people used to pray for their needs and wants, but now it seems they borrow instead of pray. An appropriate bumper sticker, to reflect the unconscious attitude of many of God's people, would be, *Why Pray When You Can Borrow?*

One very real disappointment in recent years has been the increase in churches and ministries that have gone into debt. People used to believe that if God directed, He would provide. They would fast and pray and wait for God to provide. Now they don't have to do that, they can go to the bank or to the bond company for their provision. No wonder the power of God is missing.

People explain away the biblical admonition of Romans 13:8, *"Owe no man anything, but to love one another..."*

Proverbs 22:26 says: *"Be not thou one of them that strike hands, or one of them that are sureties for debts."*

Them that strike hands, refers to a person entering into a debt agreement. *Them that are sureties for debts*, are those who provide security for a debt, often called a cosigner.

Proverbs 17:18 says: *"A man void of understanding striketh hands, and becometh surety in the presence of a friend."*

Again the Scriptures warn against going into debt or providing security for a debt.

In speaking with my Jewish friend, I told him there are Christians who believe it is all right to go in debt for some things. He said, "That is typical of you Gentiles, making a decision based on what is profitable, rather than on what God's Word says is right."

You Can't Serve Two Masters
(Matt. 6:19-24)

Jesus told us we must be careful how we handle our finances or we may find our finances exerting a control on our lives. He gave a very strong warning in the gospel of Matthew.

"Lay not up for yourselves treasures upon earth, where moth and rust doth corrupt, and where thieves break through and steal: But lay up for yourselves treasures in heaven, where neither moth nor rust doth corrupt, and where thieves do not break through and steal: For where your treasure is there will your heart be also" (Matt. 6:19-21).

"No man can serve two masters: for either he will hate the one, and love the other; or else he will hold to the one and despise the other. Ye cannot serve God and mammon (money)" (Matt. 6:24).

Jesus is warning that unless we are careful, money will persuade us to serve it. He follows His warning with a very absolute statement: it is not possible to serve both God and money. There is no middle ground. Either you serve God or the monetary system of this world.

I have seen people who thought they could serve both God and money, only to find themselves sidetracked from accomplishing His will. I knew a former vice-president of a Christian college who resigned from the college so he could make a lot of money in a multilevel marketing company. His goal was to make enough money in a few years so he could help the college without having to draw a salary. It was a noble goal, but that was many years ago and he never did fulfill his goal.

Many people do not intend to serve money, but end up doing so. It happens over and over again. One of the dangers of going into debt is that you get placed in the position of having to serve money. Proverbs 22:7 says, *"The rich ruleth over the poor, and the borrower is servant to the lender."*

Beware of the snares money will set before you. If you are ensnared, apply the principles of God's Word and break free from those bonds and serve the Lord anew. Remember God is a much better master than finances will ever be (Ps. 68:19).

You Must Pay All Your Debts
(Ps. 37:21; Eccl. 5:4; Prov. 6:1-5)

Although God does not want you to go in debt, if you are in debt, He expects you to pay all your debts. Psalm 37:21 says, *"The wicked borroweth, and payeth not again: but the righteous sheweth mercy and giveth."*

You must pay that which you owe. Even if you got into a situation you shouldn't be in and owe money you shouldn't owe, you must pay it off. You must think very carefully before putting yourself in such a situation again (Eccl. 5:4-5).

The Bible not only tells us to pay our debts but it also tells us to do it as soon as possible. Consider the teaching of Proverbs 6:1-15. The person who is in debt or who has provided security for a debt is snared (v.1-2). They must humble themselves and see that the debt is paid off (v.3). This repayment must be made as soon as possible. It may even require staying up late and using our rest time to work overtime or to take a second job (v.4, 9-15).

There should be a real urgency to get out of debt. It may take cautious determination, like the deer who discovers a hunter on its trail. That deer will call upon its God-given instincts for survival and will cautiously investigate every possible means of escape, then quickly and quietly pursue the best route out. Or it may take an all-out concentrated effort like the bird who sits upon its branch waiting for the hunter to pass, only to discover the hunter is drawing nearer. It waits for the last possible minute, then with every ounce of energy it can muster, it boldly and quickly flutters away (v. 5).

The best thing to do is stay out of debt. If you are in debt, get out of debt as soon as possible. God does not want you in debt, for your sake, for His sake, and for the sake of those who need to see Him in you.

How to Experience Debt-Free Living

If you are in debt you need to take some practical steps to apply these principles.

Commit Your Finances to God
(2 Cor. 9:8)

God can get you out of debt. He can provide so you can have your needs met, your debts paid off, and your resources abounding. But you must first make the commitment to follow His principles and allow Him to have His will and way in your life. This can be done as a simple prayer, right now, with the right heart attitude.

Restructure Your Life

"By humility and the fear of the Lord are riches, honour, and life" (Prov. 22:4).

There are two important principles from Proverbs 22:4, that you must apply to your situation if you want to get out of debt. They are *humility* and *the fear of the Lord.*

1. *Humility.* The type of humility God seeks is very practical. He wants you to take a good hard look at your situation, admit what is wrong, and accept responsibility for it.

One way to see where you really are financially, is to take a *Personal Financial Inventory.* It will become a tool to help you take the steps to make changes God wants in your life.

Another important step you need to take is to determine a *Workable Budget.* A lot of people balk at the idea of having a budget. That is where humility comes in. Accept the fact that you need to determine some type of practical guidelines to direct your spending according to God's order in finances. A carefully and prayerfully prepared budget will help you do that.

You will also need humility to change your buying habits. You must pray about each expenditure (1 Thess. 5:17).

If you want to get out of debt, you must stop going into debt any further. Stop using credit cards, store charges, and lay-a-way, and start to pray-a-way your debts instead.   Another step that will help you get out of debt, but which also requires humility, is learning to do do-it-yourself jobs. Learn how to use the self-serve pumps when you get gasoline for your car, instead of using the full-serve pump. Self-service often costs considerably less. Learn to change the oil in your car. Learn to do simple repairs around home. There are a host of ways you can save money and reduce your expenses through do-it-yourself jobs.

Another step which requires humility, is learning how to economize. You need to learn how to shop wisely and economically. You'll get more for your grocery dollar if you learn to make out a grocery list, look at the sale papers, use coupons, and plan out your shopping route so you don't drive unnecessary miles.

There are hundreds of ways to economize. Talk with others and discuss some ways they have learned to economize. Remember it takes humility to do this. Would you buy the no-frills-brand items, that are often just as good as the name-brand items, to save money?

2. *Fear of the Lord.* The other important ingredient you need to get out of debt is the *fear of the Lord.* Acknowledge that you and all you own belongs to the Lord. Make all financial decisions in light of His Word. Remember, you are a steward of that which is His. Use it His way.

Learn to Be Content
(1 Tim. 6:6-10)

It seems that contentment is one of the hardest things to learn. We always want more than we have. If you are going to get out of debt, you must learn the principle of contentment.

1. Remember that God promises to provide all your needs.

2. Learn to discern the difference between "needs" and "wants."

3. Don't forget to express thankfulness. You may not be out of debt yet, but there is still so much to thank God for. He delights in a thankful people.

Tithe, Give the Firstfruits
(Mal. 3:9)

Start to follow God's order in finances and give God the tithe (firstfruits). This is your number one financial commitment.

If you have not done this before, you may find it hard at

first, but the rest of the program falls apart if you neglect this step.

The best way to do this is to set aside the money for your tithe as soon as any income comes in. It will soon become a spiritual habit.

Provide for Your Family's Needs
(1 Tim. 5:8)

One of the first areas we violate when we are in debt is the area of meeting our family's needs. God says you must not violate this area.

Meeting your family's needs comes before paying off debts. If your debt repayments are so large you cannot meet the basic needs of your family, you must increase your income or reduce your debt load. If additional income is not an option for you and you can not liquidate (pay off) some of your debts so you can meet your family's needs, you need to look at extending the term of payment on your debts. This will reduce the amount of your regular payments.

You must be sure your family has adequate food and clothing. These are budget priorities. God said He would provide them with those things. Do not deny them. If it comes down to the choice between putting food on the table or paying a past-due bill, be sure the food is on the table. Do not compromise your family's other needs like shelter, heat, medical needs, and even some conservative recreation.

Get Out of Debt Now
(Prov. 6:1-5)

Take some practical steps to get out of debt now.

Analyze Your Present Debts. Make a list of all the money you owe to anyone. Don't forget your charge cards, bank loans, school bills, past-due payments, and personal loans. A debt listing sheet is a helpful tool for this.

Restructure Your Finances. Change the way you conduct your financial affairs to conform with biblical principles and God's order in finances. If you do not have a checking account, open one. This will help you keep a better log and control on your spending. Use only one checkbook for an account and keep it up to date, both balanced and reconciled.

Start Using a Written Budget. Prayerfully and carefully prepare your written budget, then stick by it. Its purpose is to guide your spending, not just keep track of it.

Use an easy system to monitor and maintain your budget (i.e., the "Christian Budget Bookkeeping System").

Start a Repayment Plan. Under your guideline budget, determine what you should spend on debt repayment. Make sure each person on your debt listing sheet is paid something regularly. If you have been delinquent on your payments or if you have to reduce the regular payment amount for one or more parties, send them a letter. In the letter you may want to tell them you have undertaken a study of the *Biblical Principles of Finances* and have begun to take some practical steps to eliminate your debts and keep from getting further in debt. Apologize for your delinquency or reduction in your payment, but assure them of your intention to stick to your budget and repayment schedule.

Start a Savings Plan. Remember the ant from the book of Proverbs. Start a savings plan. Designate a regular amount, even if it is only a couple of dollars, and set it aside for an emergency fund. This can be done with your budget and put in your checking account until you have enough to open a savings account or to invest in another vehicle that provides you easy access to your money.

Stop Procrastinating or Speculating

"Boast not thyself of tomorrow; for thou knowest not what a day may bring forth" (Prov. 27:1).

Don't wait until tomorrow to make the changes you need to make. There is never a better time to start doing right, than right now.

Don't live on potential income. That is speculating. Too many people spend money before it comes in, assuming it will be there. They use methods like post-dating checks, using lay-a-way at the department store or spending the amount allocated for the rent or mortgage on something else, expecting to make it up from the next paycheck. Wait until you have the funds before you spend them.

Another important thing to do is to consider the ant principle from the book of Proverbs and begin to prepare for tomorrow, today. Have you set up your savings account yet? Do you have a retirement fund? Have you begun to set aside an inheritance for your children and grandchildren? Don't wait any longer.

Avoid "Get Rich Quick" Solutions
(Prov. 20:21; 28:8; Jer. 17:11)

There is a tendency for people to want to get out of debt so bad, that they look for *Get Rich Quick* schemes rather than applying the principles from God's Word.

Don't Use Any Wrong Methods of Gain. You should not violate one biblical principle so you can fulfill another one. That never works. Lotteries, betting on the horses, and all other forms of gambling certainly do not have their place in a Christian's life. Refrain from the many things that are wrong for a Christian to do to earn money.

Don't use any questionable methods of gain. Some areas of gain are not specifically prohibited by the Bible, but they are questionable. If they are questionable, be sure to avoid them.

Don't use efforts that produce without proportionate effort. There are many multilevel marketing schemes that promise lots of money for little or no effort. The Bible says to watch out for the person who talks instead of works. Beware of other business schemes and investments which promise a quick return without some type of proportionate effort.

Stop Impulse Buying or Self-Gratification

*"And besides this, giving all diligence, add to your faith virtue; and to your virtue knowledge; and to knowledge **temperance** (self control)..." (2 Peter 1:5-6)*

If you are used to walking into a store and buying whatever you want, you are going to have to make a change. Until you get out of debt, you must let your budget be a guide for your purchases. You must put an end to impulse buying or self-gratification.

Set guidelines for purchases according to biblical principles and your current financial situation. Perhaps you should set a dollar limit on purchases, which require a family conference to exceed. Stay within your written budget and apply self-discipline and prayer.

If you want to go window shopping be sure to leave your checkbook and charge cards at home.

Apply Diligence
(Prov. 14:23; Gen. 1:15; 3:17-19)

There is no easy way to get out of debt. The only way you are going to get out of debt and stay out of debt, is to diligently apply the biblical principles of finances.

Don't expect anyone to hand you an easy way out. If they do, it is probably the wrong way. You will have to work hard before you see the first few rays of sun at the end of your tunnel, but the darkest hours mean dawn is just in sight.

There will be times when you will feel like quitting. In those times pray and remember who you are serving. Set your eyes on the joy that is before you. Run the race and do not quit. There is a prize waiting for you.

For Review and Reflection...

1. Why is how you handle your finances important?

2. What are some reasons people are in debt?

3. Why does God want you to be a lender, not a borrower?

4. Is it possible to walk the fence and serve God *and* money?

5. What are the two important principles in Proverbs 22:4?

6. What are the practical steps necessary to get out of debt now?

Chapter Five
ESTABLISHING AND MAINTAINING
A WORKABLE BUDGET

You Can Develop a Workable Budget

This is where we come to the real nuts and bolts of applying the biblical principles of finances. Establishing a workable budget is not an easy job, but it can be done. It provides you with a major tool to use to apply the biblical principles of finances to your life. Learning how to use that tool will help you to experience financial freedom. It is a spiritual task which you can do with God's help by prayerfully and carefully following the advice in this chapter.

Have you ever tried to put together a budget? Without some practical advice it can be a frustrating experience. Some who have tried it, cringe at the idea. Others avoid budgeting because it seems like such a complex and insurmountable task.

Many times in the past I was frustrated as I tried to put together a budget for my family. I purchased various budget books and followed the instructions step by step. Each time I was disappointed as I found them either too overwhelming or too impractical.

Most of those books had three deficiencies in common. First, they had you track your spending for a month or two, writing down every expenditure. This gives you a picture of where you are, which is helpful. The problem though, is that you wait another month to bring your finances under control. You do not receive any immediate relief from the financial pressures you are under. Many people who try that method, never make it through the first month of the program.

Second, they have you determine a new budget based on the data you compiled. The problem with that is, your budget gets based on your spending patterns, not on biblical principles.

Third, the budget they have you develop is geared to record your spending, not guide or control it. It becomes a source for further evaluation, recording what you have spent, rather than a control to determine what you spend.

What you need is a workable budget which is not complex or impractical. It needs to be developed in a short period of time, must be based upon biblical principles, and should serve as a personal guide to help you experience financial freedom.

The goal of this chapter is to help you develop that kind of budget and to help you see how to maintain the budget once it is developed. Remember, establishing a workable budget is only half the battle. Putting that budget into practice on a daily basis, when confronted by the realities and complexities of life, is the other half.

Determine Why You Should Have a Written Budget

You must give an account before God of how you handle your finances (1 Cor. 4:1-2; Luke 16:10-11; 2 Cor. 5:10). The word *account* is a financial term. Your written budget will help you give a better account of how you handle your finances and will also help you achieve your goals. It helps you become the master of your finances, rather than your finances becoming your master (Matt. 6:24).

A written budget can enable you to have surplus from which you may give to help meet the needs of others or from which you can acquire some of the things you desire (2 Cor. 9:8).

A written budget will also help you to get out of debt and stay out of debt.

Determine Your Budget

If you are married, you should work on this section together as a family. The way you handle your finances is a family matter that affects every member in your household.

Write Out a List of Goals

What are your goals? What do you want to accomplish with

your life? Too often people have allowed finances to control their lives. Many people are so busy earning a living that they never have time to live. Their main goal in life is to exist.

There is more to life than just working and earning a living. God wants you to experience the joy of living for Him. You can glorify God and know His power and victory in your life, but you need to set some goals to do that (1 John 1:4; 1 Cor. 10:32).

Life is like a race. In a race, the runners set their eyes on the goal – the finish line – then direct all of their energy to reach that goal. You must determine what your finish line is. Where is your goal? Then set your eyes on that goal and run for it (Phil. 3:12-14; Heb. 12:1-2).

Write out some long-term goals. Think about the future. What do you want to accomplish in the course of your life? Where do you want to be when it comes time to take your last breath? What about retirement? What are your long-term financial goals? Don't be too general or vague. Write down specifics. Some people won't do this because they are afraid they won't accomplish what they write down. There is nothing wrong with setting a noble goal and not reaching it, as long as you give it your best and leave the results up to God. It is faithfully undertaking that journey with God, towards the goal, which marks a noble man. Too many people spend their life aiming at nothing and never know what it is to walk toward a goal with God.

Write out some short-term goals too. What do you want to accomplish in your life in the next one to five years? Again, be specific in what you write down.

God may change some of your goals. That's fine. A goal serves to get you moving for God. It gives you something to aim toward. A moving car is easier to steer than one that is sitting still. The same is true in our lives. It is easier for God to redirect someone who is moving, than it is to direct one who is sitting (Acts 16:6-10).

Complete a Personal Financial Inventory

If you are going to get where God wants you to be, it is necessary to determine where you are financially. Everyone's financial situation is unique. Take a Personal Financial Inventory. It will help you identify your regular as well as your fixed and variable expenses. With that information you can determine a budget that will work for you.

It is not essential to know where every penny, or for that matter, where every dollar, is going. But it is important to identify how much is being spent on fixed expenses like mortgage or rent and loan payments and on variable expenses like utilities, taxes, and food.

You need a reasonable picture of your average income and expenses. Fill out an Income and Expense Worksheet. Compile your figures based on your pay period.

Round off income figures to the next lowest dollar and expense figures to the next highest dollar. This is the safest method for personal budgeting. For example, if your car payment is $362.45, round it off to $363. If you are paid $525.65, round it off to $525.

If you are paid monthly – figure how much income you receive and what expenses you have on a monthly basis. Rent or mortgage payments and loan payments are usually paid monthly and are usually the same amount each month.

Many expenses are *variable* and have to be estimated. For example, utilities vary throughout the year. If you save copies of your utility bills, add up your bills for each utility for the past year. Then divide that figure by 12 to give you a monthly average for each utility.   For example, if your electric bills totaled $1,254 for the last 12 months, divide $1,254 by 12, which equals $104.50 per month.

If you did not keep a copy of your bills, go through your checkbook and add up what you paid for each utility over the past year. If you do not have your checkbook, call each utility and tell them you are putting together a budget so you can pay them promptly. Ask for the total amount you were billed by them this past year.

Some items, like taxes and auto registrations, are billed once a year. Divide those amounts by 12 to give you the monthly cost factor.

If you are paid weekly – you need to convert all your expenses to weekly items, so you know what they cost you each week. Some people make the mistake of dividing each month into four weeks when they figure a budget. If there were four weeks in each month there would only be 48 weeks in the year. Beware of that mistake. There are 52 weeks in a year and more than four weeks in a month.

To determine how much a monthly bill costs on a weekly basis, multiply it times 12. That will give you the annual cost. Then divide that figure by 52 to get a weekly cost.

For example, if your mortgage is $800 per month, multiply $800 x 12 = $9,600 per year. Then divide $9,600 by 52 = $185 per week.

Establish a Debt Repayment Plan

If your debt payments are greater than 5 percent of your net spendable income, refer to the Workbook section, "How to Achieve Debt Repayment."

Develop a New Budget

After you have completed a Personal Financial Inventory, follow these steps:

Compare What You Currently Spend. First compare what you spend, with what others who have the same income spend, then what others with the same size family spend. Those figures are based on actual nationwide figures, but are not based on biblical principles.

Next, compare what you spend with the Suggested Spending Guidelines. Everyone's situation is slightly different and yours will vary from those suggested. Keep in mind that the figures have been drafted to serve as a guideline to help you determine a new budget based on God's principles. Consider bringing as many of your figures in line with the guidelines as possible. When you allow a higher figure in one area it will require a lower figure somewhere else. Make such changes prayerfully and carefully.

Consider Ways to Reduce Expenses or Increase Income. If your expenses are greater than your income you must make some changes. Remember, *"If your outgo exceeds your income, your upkeep will become your downfall."*

There are many ways to reduce expenses. Refer to the booklet, *112 Proven Ways to Reduce Your Personal Expenses* for more than 100 proven money-saving ideas. Talk with others and ask them to share their cost-cutting methods. You will find some which will work for you. If after considering as many reductions as possible, you find your expenses are still greater than your income, consider ways to increase your income without violating biblical principles.

Carefully Determine Budget Figures. Apply the biblical principles as you determine amounts for each of the following areas:

TITHE – This should equal 10% of your gross income.

TAXES – Use the general figures from the Suggested Spending Guidelines or fill out a Tax Computation Sheet to be more specific.

NET SPENDABLE INCOME – Subtract the tithe and taxes from your total gross income. This is the figure the rest of your budget and all of the Suggested Spending Guidelines are based upon.

FOOD – 15-20% of your net income is best. Do not include eating out here; that is part of entertainment.

HOUSING – Do not exceed the guidelines. If you spend 40 percent of your net spendable income on housing, that is a danger sign.

Remember that housing includes rent or mortgage as well as taxes, insurance, utilities, and maintenance for your dwelling.

CLOTHING – Stay within the guidelines on this one. Don't overspend or underspend. Buy on a *cash only* basis. Wait for sales. Take proper care of clothing. You need good items, but you don't *need* expensive name-brand items. Teach your children contentment in this area by example. A lot of money is wasted because of extravagant tastes or caving in to peer pressure, both among adults and teens. Use good hand-me downs when possible.

TRANSPORTATION – If your existing budget exceeds the guidelines, investigate means of reduction: pay off auto loans, economize on driving, use the proper fuel, learn some "do it yourself jobs." Be sure to set aside a regular amount for a vehicle replacement fund. If your existing budget is below the guideline, save the surplus for this fund.

Avoid borrowing for car purchases. If you are making car payments, when you finish paying off the car, adjust that figure within the guidelines and put that money in the vehicle replacement fund. Maintain your old car until you save enough to buy a replacement. Only replace it when it is needed, unless you have an abundance and can purchase a want.

In some locations it is wiser to use public transportation than your own vehicle. Those costs come under this area. I knew one couple in New York City who sold their car so they did not have to make car payments, nor pay insurance and expensive parking fees. They reduced this area of their budget considerably and used the surplus to rent a nice car when they wanted to go on a trip out of the city.

MEDICAL – Use for your deductible and medications. Save the unused portion for emergencies. Shop for the best rates for medical services, medical products, and prescriptions.

ENTERTAINMENT & RECREATION – Don't neglect this area. Be sure to set aside money for vacations. Learn how to economize here. You don't have to spend a lot of money on recreation. Some forms of recreation cost very little, such as: walking, hiking, riding bicycles, going to a Little League game or attending a concert at church or school.

MISCELLANEOUS – Follow guideline percentages. This area includes all money for gifts and reasonable allowances for all family members, which gives each person a measure of financial freedom and teaches children responsibility. Help them put together a budget for their allowance and any income they earn. A good basic budget for children living at home, until they head off to college is:

10% – Tithe

50% – Long -Term Savings (College, House)

20% – Short-Term Savings (Car, Computer, Clothing)

20% – Spending Money (Entertainment, Snacks, Dates, Books, Clothing)

INSURANCE – Take into account policies provided by work. Do not over-insure. Avoid whole-life, variable life or similar policies. They often do not provide a good return on the dollar. Term insurance can save you a considerable amount and often provides a better return on the dollar, especially if you invest the difference between what you pay for term and other policies.

DEBTS – When your debt is eliminated, this amount can be used for a vehicle replacement fund, short-term purchases, missions giving or savings. Do not exceed 5 percent of your net spendable income. If you have exceeded the 5 percent guideline, only go as high as 10 percent in this area as part of a well-thought-out debt repayment plan.

SAVINGS – Even if you are in debt, you need to start saving for unforeseen events. Save something, even if just a few dollars every pay period. Get a good return on your investments (refer to the section on Savings and Investments). Set up both long-term and short-term savings. Long term should be used for retirement, inheritance, and emergencies.

Short term should be used for education, equipment purchases, wants, giving fund, etc.

TOTAL – Your total budget must not exceed your net spendable income.

Determine a System for Maintaining Your Budget

Remember your budget is a guide to help you apply the biblical principles of finances. It will not do you much good to put effort into drafting a budget if you are not going to maintain it.

The following principles will help you to put your budget to work and maintain it.

Establish a Means of Distributing Income and Expenses According to Your Budget. Your budget will not work, unless you have a written means of distributing income *to* and controlling expenses *from* each budget area. Use a simple home ledger system, like the Christian Budget Bookkeeping System, for maintaining your budget. You don't need anything complex.

The Christian Budget Bookkeeping System is called a *simplified fund accounting system* in accounting terms. It is so simple all you need to understand about finances is how to add and subtract. It is a lot like the old envelope budget system people used years ago. Under the envelope system, whenever someone received income, they had a sheet on the front where they added the amount they were putting in. They then put a portion of the money in each envelope, according to their budget.

If someone received $200, $100 might go in the rent envelope, $50 in the utilities envelope, $50 in the food envelope, $20 in the car envelope, $20 in the clothing envelope, and $10 in the miscellaneous envelope.

When someone needed to pay the rent, they went to the envelope and the money was there. When it was time to buy clothing, they went to the clothing envelope and were guided by what was there. There wasn't any overspending. That system worked great for a number of generations, and kept a lot of God-fearing people out of debt.

In our current society where many bills must be paid by check, the Christian Budget Bookkeeping System works the same way as the envelope system, except it uses a checkbook and ledger pages to record and control each budget category. It is comprised of a simple ledger and a checking account.

THE LEDGER (with two sections) –*The Checking Account Ledger* is where you record all activity from your checking account. It adds one more detail than the ledger in your checkbook in that it has a column where you identify to which budget areas the money from each deposit is distributed and from which budget area each expense is deducted. This gives you an overall picture of all income and expenses.

The Budget Account Pages. Each section in your budget is given a page, which is referred to as an account. Every time a deposit is made to the checking account, the whole amount is written on the Checking Ledger page. Then it is distributed out to different accounts, determined by your budget, just like under the envelope system. The amount of the deposit which corresponds to each budget area is added to the corresponding Budget Account page.

Every time a check needs to be written, look at the appropriate Budget Account Page to see if the funds are there. Then write the check and record it on that page, subtracting that amount. You then write it on the Checking Account Ledger, indicating from which account it was taken. This serves as a guide and a means of evaluating specific areas of expense.

THE CHECKING ACCOUNT – Open a simple checking account, preferably with no service charges and possibly with interest. This can be converted to a N.O.W. (Negotiable Orders of Withdrawal) Account or to a Super N.O.W. Account for better interest as balances accumulate in the various accounts. Be sure to use only one checkbook per checking account.

Limit All Distribution of Income to Your Written Budget. Develop the habit of using your prayerfully prepared budget as your guide for what you spend, not your checkbook or credit card balance.

If an item is on sale, and it is something you need or want, look at your budget to see if the money is there in that category to spend.

If you have an emergency and funds are not available in a certain account, you need to see if you can transfer funds from one account to another. It would be better to borrow from yourself this way, than to use a credit card or get a loan where you have to pay interest.

Revise the Budget Periodically. You will undoubtedly have to make changes to your budget from time to time. Be flexible in making changes if they are needed, but make those changes prayerfully and carefully.

Eliminate the Use of Credit Cards as Much as Possible. Credit cards can be real budget busters. They are difficult to control. They can be helpful under some circumstances as long as you pay off the balance due. If you use credit cards, be sure you do not exceed your budget balances as you purchase items.

Avoid Carrying Cash, Except for Certain Purposes. Most people have a tendency to spend cash on hand and have a hard time accounting for it. Remember God says we will give an account for how we handle all our money.

If you want to carry some spending money with you, be sure to budget it. Allowances are a good source for spending money. You may need to carry cash for gasoline, public transportation, eating out, and groceries. Remember to budget those items. You may want to carry a miniature envelope system with you as a control.

Record All Expenditures in Your Ledger Book. Don't slack off and stop recording your expenditures in your Ledger Book. It is a hard habit to develop at first but just a few minutes each day and the task will be done. The benefits of using such a system will outweigh any inconvenience it may cause at first.

Amounts for Giving Gifts and Special Needs (Church, Family, Friends, etc.) Are Regulated by Your Budget. Gift giving and giving to special needs can really blow a budget to pieces. You must remember to consider amounts for these two areas as you prayerfully prepare your budget. Look at the balances available in those categories before you spend funds.

One reason to have a budget is to help you reach the place where you will be able to give more to special needs. Don't let your emotions guide you in this area. Use prayer and your budget.

Remember the example of the Corinthians (1 Cor. 16:1-4). A need was made known and they budgeted a portion in advance each week, until they had the funds to help meet the need.

Let Jesus Be the Lord of Your Budget. Don't Let Your Budget Be Your Lord.

Variables to Consider with Your First Budget

When you put together your first budget, according to the biblical principles of finances, always figure out a model budget based on the guidelines recommended in the chapter "Establishing and Maintaining a Workable Budget." Take into account that bills have accumulated while you have not budgeted for them. If taxes are due in September and you start your budget in January and don't make any adjustments in your budget, you will not have enough money to pay the taxes from your tax account when the bill comes due in September. You will be behind by 13 weeks. The same applies for utilities for approaching heating and cooling systems, auto insurance, and a number of other variable (quarterly or annual) bills.

There are two ways to deal with this problem:

If you have an abundance set aside – you can take a portion of it and make up for the number of weeks you missed budgeting each item, since your last major payment. Then begin the regular pay period allotment to each area. For example, if you are paid on a weekly basis and figure it cost you $1,200 for heating bills last year, you would budget $24 per week. If you started budgeting that much at the end of the last heating season you would be able to pay this season's bills because a surplus would have accumulated during the off season, when the bills were lower. If you started budgeting 15 weeks after the end of the last heating season, you would have to make an adjustment because you would be 15 weeks behind in that account. To solve the deficiency, calculate your weekly heating bill budget figure, then multiply it times 15 and put that much aside in your utilities fund. In this case, it would be $24 x 15 = $360.

If you do not have an abundance set aside – you will have to readjust some of your budget figures until the variable payments are complete or the annual payments have been paid. For example, using the above illustration, you would have to come up with the $1,200 for the approaching heating system in 37 weeks (52 weeks -15 weeks = 37 weeks). You would then have to divide $1,200 by 37 weeks to come up with your adjusted budget figure, which would equal $33 per week.

If you start your budget in the middle of the heating system, determine how many weeks are left until the largest heating bill comes due. Total all the bills you anticipate by that date and divide the number of pay periods left between now and then to arrive at your budget heating amount.

For example, if you start your budget in January and the largest heating bill is the March one which comes due in April, estimate how much the total of all the bills will be until then. If the bill due in February is $150; March is $200; and April is $250, you need a total of $600. If you have 13 weeks to come up with that amount, you will need to set aside $47 per week. After the heating season ends you can replace that figure with the one in your original budget.

For Review and Reflection...

1. What are some things a written budget will do for you?

2. Have you written down some long-term and short-term goals?

3. Have you taken a Personal Financial Inventory?

4. What are the steps for determining a budget?

5. Have you determined your new budget yet?

6. Why should you have some type of a budget system?

7. What are some things you can do to help maintain your budget?

8. What are some variables you must keep in mind when compiling your first budget?

Chapter Six
ABUNDANCE, INVESTMENTS, INHERITANCE, AND INSURANCE

Abundance: God's Desire for Every Believer

Too many of God's people accept less than He wants for them. God wants His people to be in the place where He can bless them with abundance, so they in turn can minister to the physical needs of others (2 Cor. 9:6-8).

Dealing with abundance presents a real challenge. Material wealth is a powerful tool. It is somewhat like a chainsaw. A chainsaw is a tool which in the right hands can accomplish a lot of good. It can easily take a load of logs and convert it into a stack of firewood. Yet the saw is powerful and dangerous and must be used with great care and respect. If it is used incorrectly it can tear through human flesh with greater ease than it tears through logs. Material wealth is like that. If you do not use it properly it will take control and tear away at your spiritual commitment.

You would never give a chainsaw to a child until the child was able to handle it. In the same way God does not give you abundance until you can handle it. There are some people who are old enough and capable enough to handle a chainsaw but who never will use one because of the potential danger it presents. Instead, they choose less efficient tools for the job. The same is true with abundance. Some are afraid to take the steps to attain that which God has for them. Perhaps the commitment or responsibility or the potential danger of misusing that which God wants to entrust to them scares them. They become like the servant who hid his talent rather than investing it. They accept less than God has for them.

We must look carefully at this area of abundance. It is a powerful tool, one which God wants you to learn how to handle. Study the principles regarding abundance, especially the section on Savings and Investments. If you understand and start to apply the principles regarding abundance now, God may be able to begin to entrust more of this precious tool to you. He needs more people today who will trust Him, apply His principles and, with His help, enter victoriously into the area of abundance. With God's help you can do it and bring glory to Him (Phil 4:13).

Basic Principles Regarding Abundance

Finances Are a Spiritual Matter
(1 Sam. 2:7; 1 Chron. 29:12; Prov. 10:22)

Remember that the way you handle your finances is a spiritual matter. Finances are one of the tests you must go through on the proving grounds of life to help you to become a more mature Christian. God's Word is full of principles to provide you with the knowledge you need to pass the test with flying colors.

The key to proper use of finances is to think of them as a tool to help you serve the Lord. He wants you in the place of abundance so you can use your finances to more effectively serve Him. Though riches can cause much grief and sorrow for those who do not apply God's principles, there is no sorrow in riches when you apply God's principles.

Abundance Is Primarily for Giving
(2 Cor. 8:14; 9:7-8)

Remember, God's main purpose for providing you with an abundance is so you will be able to serve Him more effectively and help meet the physical needs of His work and His people.

An abundance will also help you meet your wants and desires and those of your family, but the joy those material desires promise often pale in comparison as you become more actively involved in giving and meeting the needs of others.

Even though you may not have an abundance now, determine how you would like to be involved in giving to God's work and His people. Picture the joy and the benefit to God's work and His people if you were an instrument God could use bless others. He can make you abound so you can do that.

God Wants You to Serve Him with Your Abundance
(Deut. 28:47; Luke 12:13-21; 16:10-11)

Handling abundance in a way that blesses both you, your family, God's work, and His people takes wisdom. Riches have sidetracked many to their hurt and shame. God needs more people who seek His wisdom in handling their finances so He can bless them with an abundance.

One day Solomon was given the chance to ask God for anything. Can you imagine being given the chance to ask for one wish that you knew would be granted? Solomon could have asked for long life, for his enemies to be defeated or for great riches. But he did not ask for any of those things. Instead he asked God to give him wisdom. God answered the request and gave Solomon wisdom; but He also gave him long life, victory over his enemies, and great wealth (1 Kings 3:5-14). You need to ask God for wisdom too (James 1:5-8).

It also takes faithfulness to serve God with your abundance. As a steward of what God has entrusted to you, you must be faithful (1 Cor. 4:1).

Warnings Regarding Abundance

There are a number of warnings to heed when you come to the place of abundance.

Watch out for a Superior Attitude
(Prov. 18:23; 28:11).

Sometimes a person with an abundance may think he or she attained it because he or she is better or smarter than others. Sometimes the person may look down on those who do not have an abundance and treat them poorly.

Watch Out for Trusting Riches Instead of God
(Ps. 52:7).

Sometimes people trust what is in their bank account to see them through tough times rather than trusting God, when He actually provided the bank account so they could be prepared.

Beware of Serving Money
(Luke 16:13).

Money will try to get you to serve it. It will attempt to become a priority in your life and take a lot of your time.

Riches and Cares Can Sidetrack You
*(Luke 8:14).

Be careful that acquiring or maintaining your abundance does not divert you from serving God. This happens too often.

Money Can Steal Your Heart
(Luke 12:29-34).

Be careful that you do not fall in love with your abundance. Money and material things can steal your heart. Are you willing to leave all your goods and possessions for Christ? Remember, where your treasure is, there will your heart be also.

Savings and Investments: Using God's Money Wisely

God expects you to be a wise steward of all He entrusts to you. Follow the example of the ant in Proverbs 6:6-11. Learn to apply the principles of saving wisely.

Biblical Principles Regarding Savings and Investments

God Blesses Diligence
(Prov. 10:4-5).

If you want to experience the abundance God wants for you then you must do it His way. His Word teaches us that He wants us to work for what He wants to give us. He blesses hard work, not "Get Rich Quick" solutions.

The Wise Man Saves
(Prov. 21:20).

Too many times when people get more than they need, they spend the extra on their wants rather than save it. The wise man sets aside a portion of what he earns.

Provide Now for Hard Times
(Prov. 6:6-8).

Hard times are going to come. You will have unexpected illness and things you need are going to break down and need repair or replacement. You must discipline yourself to save and prepare for those hard times. No matter how little you earn, save *something*.

This also applies to preparing for your retirement. There will be a day when you cannot work. Begin to prepare now so you do not become a burden to your children or grandchildren.

Invest and Use Your Abundance Wisely
(Luke 19:12-22).

All investments are not wise. You must learn what are the best ways to invest the abundance God has entrusted to you. This takes wisdom.

Do not hoard the abundance God gives you. Remember to invest your abundance so you can use it. Learn how much to save and how much to distribute.

Living wills, trusts, annuities, and endowments are ways to insure that your abundance is used wisely, even after you are no longer around.

Don't Make Money on God's People or Program
(Ex. 22:25; Ezek. 18:8-9; Ps. 15:5; Prov. 28:8).

Christians should not take advantage of other Christians. Under the Old Testament Law, God forbade His people to charge each other interest. He said it was all right to charge others interest but not His people. We should follow that standard today.

God's people should not loan to each other or to God's program with interest. If you have the funds to meet a valid need, either give it as an outright gift or loan it without interest. It may not make sense financially to the world, but since when do we let the world dictate what is right and wrong?

God Can Restore a Bad Investment
(2 Chron. 25:9; Gen. 31:7).

You will likely make some decisions with your abundance which are not the best choices. You may even lose some of your abundance because of the dishonesty, misrepresentation or downfall of others. Do not lose heart. God is still in control. Be faithful to His principles and allow Him to take care of the matter for you (Rom. 8:28).

Why Should a Christian Save Money?

To Generate More Income to Give

If you carefully begin to save a portion of what you have, you will not only have more to meet your needs, but you will also have more from which to give.

If you are unable to give more than your tithe, because of your present financial situation, you could designate the interest (which you earn maintaining your basic budget with the Christian Budget Bookkeeping System) and set up a fund for giving.

If you are in the place of abundance now, you can set up a Giving Reserve Fund from which you withdraw funds as special needs come up. Without such a fund, if a missionary came to your church and presented the need for a computer for translation work, you would probably not be able to do much to help. If you had set up a Giving Reserve Fund and set aside money on a regular basis you would be able to have a greater part and possibly meet the need entirely.

To Save for Short-Term and Intermediate Needs and Variable Expenses

Paying utility bills and maintaining, repairing or replacing appliances and automobiles, cannot usually be done with one paycheck. You must set aside a regular portion each pay period for these accumulating expenses. Saving ahead provides you with a greater measure of financial freedom and much less stress when needs arise.

If you use a N.O.W. account or savings account for a portion of the funds set aside for these expenses, you can also earn interest on the money until it is needed.

To Save for Short-Term and Intermediate Wants

Accumulating the funds for wants such as a vacation or other items like a camper, snowmobile, etc., requires you to set something aside on a regular basis.

To Provide for Hard Times and Lean Periods

You must save ahead to be prepared for unexpected emergencies and medical expenses. Determine to set aside no less than three months of take-home pay as an Emergency Fund. The interest earned on it can be added to your Giving Reserve Fund.

The Emergency Fund should never be used on wants, only on emergencies. This will help prepare you for a job slow down or strike, the crushing effects of inflation, recession or economic depression.

To Provide for Retirement

You must prepare for retirement. You will never live securely on Social Security. Take some definite steps to set aside a retirement fund. If you are an employee, find out specifically what your employer provides. Will it be sufficient? If you are self-employed set up a retirement account now.

To Provide for Children and Grandchildren

Savings enables you to be actively involved in the lives of your children and grandchildren. By careful planning, you can help meet the needs and wants in their lives. You can set aside funds that will multiply and could perhaps help pay for their education, down payment on a home or fulfill some of their wants and desires. What a blessing to see the funds come from God through you. You will need a combination of investments and insurance to be able to do this.

Using Savings Wisely

Let Your Money Work for You

Years ago some people put money under their mattress or in a cookie jar to save it. That is not a good idea today, for three reasons: *Theft, Inflation,* and *Biblical Teaching.*

Theft is becoming more of a problem as our society becomes more godless. Many families have been affected by theft. My family has experienced theft both living in the city, the suburbs, and in the country.

Another reason to avoid the mattresses or cookie jars is because they eat money. The buying power of your money, stashed away in the cookie jar, constantly declines and is eaten up by *inflation* (the reduced buying power of money caused by various economic factors). Consider $100 put in a cookie jar for one year versus $100 put in a savings account yielding only 5 percent interest compounded monthly. Lets assume a modest 5 percent annual inflation rate: At the end of the year the $100 stashed in the cookie jar is worth $100 minus the 5 percent inflation ($5). That $100 minus the $5 for inflation equals $95 of buying power. The $100 in the savings account has become $105.11, less 5 percent inflation ($5.26). Take the $105.11 and subtract the $5.26 inflation and you have $99.85 of buying power.

Though theft and inflation are good reasons not to use the cookie jar for your savings, the best reason is because of the *biblical teaching* which says God wants you to put your money to work (Luke 19:12-22).

People will pay you to use your money. They will pay you *interest* (rent) on your money. Many factors affect how much interest they will pay. To be a good steward, find the best way to put your money to work.

Invest Wisely

All investments are not wise. That has been seen by the number of savings and loans and banks which have gone out of business. Prayerfully and carefully consider any investment, no matter how safe it seems.

It is a good to seek advice on investments from a knowledgeable third party. An investment broker, insurance agent or banker who wants your funds may not the best person to get advice from. They are salespeople who only earn money if you invest with them. Find some godly counselors who are familiar with investments before you place your funds in any investment.

If someone offers you a deal which is only available if you sign at that time, do not sign. If something is a good investment it can wait until you get counsel or check it out.

Don't forget to check the references of any investment you are considering.

Don't Allow Your Investments to Consume Your Time

You can spend a lot of time checking out investments and seeing that the ones you choose are performing well. Don't allow your investments to consume your time. Set a specific amount of time in your schedule for monitoring your investments and for making new investments.

Avoid "Get Rich Quick" Schemes.

There are many "Get Rich Quick" schemes out there besides lotteries and gambling. Multilevel marketing schemes, unbelievable entry-level investments, insider tips, and much more are all vying for your time and money. God does not bless *quick* income. Be sure there is a *proportionate amount of work or investment* to justify any great gain which is offered.

Some investments offer valid substantial returns, but require capital investment *and* hard work to succeed. Don't be one of the many people who lose a lot of time and money on "Get Rich Quick" schemes.

Be Careful with Speculation

Speculation is part of doing business and making investments. Almost all investments involve some measure of speculation.

People used to think putting their money in a bank was a sure thing. After hundreds of banks have closed, that thinking has changed. Investing in a bank involves speculation too.

Some investments are more conservative and involve less speculation than others. Usually the lower the rate of risk involved with an investment, the lower the rate of return.

Remember there is the possibility with some investments that you could lose all you invest. This has happened to many people. You could also get hit by a car walking across the street. That too has happened to many people. There are some chances you take after calculating the risks.

Don't Forget about Inflation and Cost-of-Living Increases

Try to do better than the rate of inflation with your investments. If you don't invest or if you invest at a rate of return which is lower than the rate of inflation, you lose buying power because inflation eats away at the buying power of your money. Most passbook savings barely keep even with inflation. Try to find an investment rate of return which is better than the rate of inflation.

Always Get the Best Interest Rate

Interest is the rent someone pays you for using your money. Different investment vehicles pay different rents.

There are basically two different types of interest: *Simple Interest* and *Compound Interest.*

Simple Interest is interest paid only on the principal (the amount you invest). For example, $500 placed in an investment and left for five years at 10 percent simple interest, will produce as follows: 10 percent interest ($50) will be added to the principal ($500) each year for five years. At the end of five years you will have: $50 x 5 = $250 interest + $500 principal = $750 total.

Compound Interest is interest paid on both the principal and accumulated interest. For example, $500 placed in an investment and left for five years at 10 percent interest compounded yearly, will produce as follows:

Year 1: 10 percent interest ($50) will be added to the principal ($500). That is $500 principal + $50 interest = $550 new principal.

Year 2: 10 percent interest ($55) will be figured on the new principal ($550). That amount will then be added to the principal: $550 principal + $55 interest = $605 new principal.

This procedure is continued for each of the five years. Each year the interest is added to the principal, then interest is calculated on the new figure. At the end of five years your $500 will have become $805.26. It would earn $55.26 more than if it had earned only simple interest.

When you are dealing with the same percentage rates, compound interest is always more beneficial than simple interest.

There are different methods for *compounding* interest (adding the interest to the principal). Some investments compound interest *yearly*. Others compound it *semi-annually* (twice a year); *quarterly* (four times a year); *monthly*; or *daily*. Daily compounding is usually figured as though each month had 30 days.

Notice the different *return* (what you end up with at the end of your investment period) in the following example:

$500 invested for a 10-year period at 10 percent will return:

$1,000.00 - with simple interest
$1,296.87 - compounded yearly
$1,326.49 - compounded semi-annually
$1,342.53 - compounded quarterly
$1,353.52 - compounded monthly
$1,362.12 - compounded daily

Shop for the Best Investments

All banks are not the same and do not offer the same rates. It is a good idea to do business with two banks which offer different services and rates. If two banks offer similar services and rates, open a N.O.W. Account in the smaller bank. It is advantageous to establish a good relationship with a local bank which has the authority to make decisions on matters such as home mortgages, etc.

For some investments you will need a broker. All brokers are not the same. Be sure to check references. Talk to other customers.

Discount brokers are often the best route for the small investor. They too are not all the same.

A visit to your local library to review some financial magazines and learn more about investments is a good idea. Find one that addresses issues of interest to you. *Money Magazine* is outstanding.

Get a guide to Mutual Funds, a report on tax law changes, or other investment summaries before making an investment. Many of these items are written in easy-to-understand language. On the other hand a *prospectus* (the legal detailed offering of an investment, approved by the state Attorney General's office) is often difficult to understand because of all the accounting and legal terminology, but should also be carefully reviewed before making an investment.

Understand the Various Types of Investments Available to You

The types of investments available to you depend on a number of factors such as: How much do you have to invest? For how long? How much risk are you willing to take? Become familiar with some of the different types of investment vehicles.

Understand the Principle of Liquidity

Liquid Accounts are investments which are readily converted to cash. They are accessible virtually anytime you need them. This would include money market accounts, money market mutual funds, N.O.W. or super N.O.W. accounts, and many savings accounts.

Many investments are not liquid. With *Non-Liquid* investments your money is locked in and is not available until the term of the investment is complete. This typically includes most Christmas clubs and savings plans as well as most bonds (unless you sell them and take a possible loss or gain, depending on the market).

Some investments have *excessive penalties* deducted from them if the money is withdrawn before the term expires. An example is the IRA (Individual Retirement Account).

Other investments have *small penalties* deducted from them if the money is withdrawn before the term expires. This includes C.D.s (Certificates of Deposit).

A few investments have *no penalties* if the money is withdrawn before the term expires. An example of this is EE Savings Bonds.

Real estate, which is often viewed and used as an investment, is not considered liquid. There are times when it can be readily sold, but then there are times when a property cannot be sold, except at a loss. The other factor which makes real estate a *non-liquid investment*, is the length of closing time needed to legally finalize a sale.

Determine the Length of Time You Can Invest Your Money

Short-Term Investments (30 Days to 1 Year) – These investments are used for money that needs to be accessible (i.e., Passbook or Statement Savings, N.O.W. Accounts, Credit Unions, U.S. EE Savings Bonds, C.D.s [Certificates of Deposit], Money Market Accounts, Money Market Mutual Funds, Treasury Bills, and Mutual Funds).

Intermediate Investments (1 Year to 5 Years) – These investments are relatively liquid (i.e., C.D.s, Money Market Accounts, Money Market Mutual Funds, U.S. EE Savings Bonds, Mutual Funds, Baby Bonds, Treasury Notes, Tax Certificates, Limited Partnerships.

Long-Term Investments (5 years plus) – These provide long-term security but are often not liquid. This category includes real estate, investment quality rare coins & art, IRAs (Individual Retirement Accounts), Keough (Self-employed Retirement Fund), Annuities, Zero Coupon Bonds, Corporate Bonds, Municipal Bonds, Mutual Funds, Precious Metals, Treasury Bonds, and Stocks.

Remember Tax Consequences

There are taxes on almost every type of investment. Some investments offer *tax-deferred* or *tax-exempt* income on your investment. For example, IRAs, Keoughs, Municipal Bonds, Tax-exempt Money Market Funds, Tax-exempt Mutual Funds, Public Utilities with DRP (Dividend Reinvestment Plan).

The rates on those investments are usually a little lower than non-deferred or non-exempt investment but can be advantageous depending on the tax-bracket you are in.

If you are in a lower tax bracket the taxes on interest will be minimal. If you are in a higher tax-bracket, the taxes on interest can be substantial and *tax-deferred* or *tax-exempt* investments are advantageous.

Some investments are exempt from both federal and state income taxes. Some tax-exempt funds are only exempt from state taxes. In a state with no state income tax, those investments do not offer any tax advantage.

Inheritance and Insurance: Leaving a Spiritual Legacy

Two areas often overlooked by believers today are inheritance and insurance. Every believer should takes steps to apply biblical principles regarding inheritance and insurance so they can leave behind a *spiritual legacy* as a light to those who follow in our footsteps.

Biblical Principles Regarding Inheritance and Insurance

You Cannot Take Any of Your Material Wealth with You When You Die (Eccl. 2:18)

The state will decide how to divide your belongings if you don't prepare a written plan in advance. Your family will not have as much say as you want them to. You need to prepare a *written disbursement plan* as part of your will.

God Expects You to Provide for Your Family (1 Tim. 5:8; 2 Cor. 12:14; Prov. 19:14; 13:22)

God expects us to provide for our families. That means both in life and in death. The Bible says a person who does not provide for their family has denied the faith and is worse than a person who denies the existence of God.

God expects you to work and save so your family has enough income. That means you must plan ahead for emergencies and retirement. It also means you must plan ahead for your death.

Who will provide for the needs and wants of your family after you are no longer around? Who will provide for their education? Who will raise your children if you die?

You Must Be Careful with Your Inheritance (Prov. 20:21)

You should be careful with your finances so you can leave an inheritance for your family. Remember that too large an inheritance can be disastrous for your family. Too little an inheritance would be wrong. You must determine what they need, what you should leave, and how you should leave it.

Money Will Help Provide Security, But God Must Be First (Eccl. 7:12: Prov. 10:15)

Finances help provide a defense against hard times. God expects you to prepare the best you can, but ultimate security comes from Him. Make sure your family knows that money, without God's wisdom, will not provide the most security and largest return.

Determining Life Insurance Needs

Life insurance can help fill the gap between what you have saved and what your family needs when you die.

Remember that life insurance agents are salesmen. They do not make money unless they get a sale. Never buy life insurance on the spot. Always do some comparison shopping before you buy insurance. Don't be afraid to change companies if you find a policy that does a better job meeting your family's needs.

Determine What Your Family Will Need If You Die. There are certain *lump sum payments* they will need to make, such as: funeral expenses, estate tax, lawyers fees, and debt retirement. You should also consider paying off the house and providing funds for education in the lump sum category.

Your family will also need living expenses. Determine what a new family budget would look like, without you. Remember it will be quite different than what it is now.

Determine Assets Available to Meet Those Needs. What assets do you have which can help meet those needs? Some possible assets include: insured debts, insured mortgage, investments, Social Security, and retirement benefits.

Supplement the Difference with Life Insurance. Don't accept some arbitrary figure. Carefully determine what you need. The combination of your life insurance policy and various assets should be enough to pay all the lump sum payments and to provide some money for living expenses for your family.

How much should you set aside for living expenses? Some people recommend the amount should be ten times the new living expense budget you figured out. That would enable your family to invest the money and live on the interest. Others recommend five times your new budget. Still others recommend ten times your present annual income, to allow for more to invest because of changing interest rates.

There will be a great temptation for your survivors to spend their inheritance in ways other than what you have determined will help them best. Many wolves will descend on them trying to carry away as much as they can. You can prevent this by setting up a trust to distribute your estate the way you have planned. You can also avoid a lot of inheritance taxes with a carefully prepared trust.

Don't pay too much for insurance by over insuring. The more assets you accumulate the less life insurance you need. Your savings plan does part of the job for which most people buy life insurance.

Remember life insurance is not a savings plan. Some life insurance policies couple a savings plan along with them, such as whole life, universal life, variable life and others. These are forced savings plans and often offer only a very minimal return.

Consider Helping the Lord's Work with Your Estate. Some people who have always wanted to do more for God's work in their lifetime but have been unable to, have found they can help when God calls them home. You can designate a portion of your estate to God's work in your will or estate plan. You need to designate this while you are alive. You can set up a clause in your will or set up a trust to accomplish this.

Some people who do not have dependents who need their financial help, designate their entire estate to the Lord's work. Some even set up a *Living Trust* or *Life Estate* while they are alive, so they can still enjoy their estate while at the same time allowing it to be used in the Lord's work.

Develop a Written Inheritance Plan

After you have determined a way to provide for your family upon your death, how can you be assured the income you provide will be used as you intended? You must develop a Written Inheritance (Estate) Plan. This will need to be reviewed annually.

Funeral Plans

If you do not prepare for this area, your family will have to make important economic decisions while they are grieving. At that time they will probably make decisions to spend more money on your funeral than they should. It could help bring them a little more peace of mind if they knew they were doing things the way you wanted them done.

Discuss possible arrangements in advance with your pastor and a funeral director. Keep in mind that funeral directors are salespeople with a product to sell.

Consider arranging a burial plot in advance. And be sure to put your plans in writing.

A Will

Remember that your will is a legal document. Be sure you prepare a will that conforms to your state laws. It is a good opportunity to leave a written spiritual legacy behind. It is a public document and may be read by genealogists and other family members for years to come.

A will consists of the following parts:

1. *Introductory Paragraph*. This is where you identify yourself. Include a brief family history. Don't forget to include your personal testimony in such a way that it clearly contains the Gospel, so someone reading it could get saved.

In this section you also need to include provisions such as:

Who will serve as guardians for your children?

How will your debts be paid off?

How will funeral expenses be paid?

How will expenses be paid to administer your estate?

2. *Legacies*. This is where you dispose of your personal property. You may designate various items for various individuals.

3. *Devices*. This is where you dispose of real property. Specific parcels may be designated for specific parties. Charitable contributions are often included here.

4. *Residuary Clause.* This is where you dispose of any property not mentioned under legacies and devices. This is usually done by designating percentages.

5. *Executors.* This is where you name legal representatives to carry out the instructions in your will. It is often a good idea to have a local bank or attorney named to handle the financial matters, rather than a relative.

6. *Signature Lines.* This is where you, the testor, signs. You should identify your physical and mental condition and residence at the time of signing.

There must also be spaces for witnesses to sign. The witnesses must identify who they are and where they live. They should be people who do not receive any inheritance in the will.

Letters of Advice

You should prepare letters in advance, advising your spouse or family what to do in the event of your death. Date this, in case you prepare revised editions later. Be sure more than one person has these. Your pastor would be a good person to give one copy to.

You may want this kept sealed with instructions to open it upon your death or serious illness.

Do not put this in a safe deposit box at a bank, because they are sealed when you die, until the time your will is executed.

Include a list of advisors that you recommend the family contact. Include a pastor and Christian lawyer.

State your desire for any funeral plans.

Consider including a letter with an appeal for others to trust Christ, which could be read at your funeral.

Trusts

Investigate the possibility of setting up a trust. Seek advice from both your pastor and a Christian attorney.

Trusts can assure that funds go where you want them. They can help avoid probate. They do not die and therefore are not taxed. They can help God's work after you and your family are gone.

Some trusts can be set up now and changed later, if needed.

For Review and Reflection...

1. What is the primary purpose for an abundance?

2. What are some warnings regarding abundance?

3. Why does God want you to save?

4. What are some things you should be saving for?

5. How can you make your money work for you?

6. What is liquidity in relation to finances?

7. Why should you have some form of insurance?

8. Why should you have a written inheritance plan?

Chapter Seven
GIVING AND KNOWING TO WHOM TO GIVE

Experience the Joy of Giving

The application of the principles contained in this section can bring a tremendous blessing to your life and to many others who reap the benefits of your obedience and love. The grace and joy of giving is an important thing that God wants every one of His children to experience. It is a way you can make a difference in lives for all eternity. Your giving can help reach souls for Christ, strengthen God's work, and help meet needs in the lives of brothers and sisters in Christ in your community and around the world. It is truly a great privilege and joy to be able to give freely.

Look carefully at what the Bible has to say about giving. Then decide how you can apply this to your life with God's help.

Understanding the Gift of Giving

Every believer has at least one spiritual gift. One gift that some people possess is the gift of giving (Rom. 12:6-8). That gift is not limited to the giving of material resources. Those with the gift of giving are sometimes able to give in miraculous ways.

Those of us who do not have the *gift* of giving can still be partakers in the *grace* of giving. As with each of the gifts of the Spirit, every believer is called upon to apply some outward function of all the other gifts. We are all called upon to do the work of the evangelist, to teach others, and to give. People who have the gift of giving will greatly abound, but we too can share in this grace.

After you give God the tithe, the rest is a grace in which you may choose to participate. It is something God wants you to cheerfully take part in with the abundance He so graciously gives you (2 Cor. 9:7).

Biblical Areas of Giving for the Believer Today

Firstfruits (Tithe)
(Prov. 3:9-10)

By giving God the first tenth (firstfruits) of all He gives you, you acknowledge His lordship in your life. If you withhold and do not honor God with the tithe, it throws a monkey wrench in the works as you seek to apply the rest of the financial principles (Mal. 3:7-9). God knows what is best for you, so follow His order in finances and put the tithe first. He wants all believers to honor Him with the firstfruits.

The firstfruits (tithe) is your first financial commitment. It does not come from your abundance. It does not come from what is left over. It comes first before everything else.

Offering
(1 Cor. 16:2)

Though the tithe is required, the offering is what you decide to give God in addition to your tithe (2 Cor. 9:7). You can set aside a portion of your abundance to meet the needs of God's work and of His people (2 Cor. 9:6).

Your tithe should be given from all income you receive but an offering should only be given if you have paid off your debts (Prov. 6:1-5). When you are in debt, a portion of your income belongs to someone else and you cannot give to God what does not belong to you.

Perhaps the portion of income you are using now to pay off your debts, can become your offering portion when your debts are eliminated. Your offering should be used to meet the needs of both your local church and God's work around the world (1 Cor. 16:1).

Sacrificial Giving
(Heb. 13:16)

There is a difference between an offering and a sacrifice

(Eph. 5:2). Sacrificial giving is doing without something you want in order to give to an important need (2 Cor. 8:1-5).

Giving sacrificially is a matter of free choice. It comes from the area of abundance, specifically from funds designated for our wants.

Fasting
(Acts 13:2-3)

Fasting is often thought of only in relation to doing without food. That is not the full intent of the word. Fasting literally means *to do without something you need*. This is one aspect of giving in which some people participate when they say they are sacrificing.

If you are in debt and desire to give more to God's work or to meet the needs of His people, fasting is the means you can use to do that. You can determine to do without something you need in order to meet someone else's needs (Isa. 58:6-7).

This is a voluntary matter. You may personally make the decision to fast but you should not make your family do this (1 Cor. 7:5). They must freely choose to participate in this grace. This is also a spiritual exercise – not to impress God, but to strengthen yourself spiritually (Ps. 35:13).

Perhaps you can designate a meal, or a day, when you set aside what you would have spent on that meal and designate it to meeting a need for God's work. Then you can dedicate the mealtime to prayer and have some real spiritual food (John 4:3-8, 25-34).

Fasting is not cutting your food budget to pay bills or to purchase wants. That violates God's principles.

Faith-Promise Giving

There are a lot of different teachings around about what has come to be known as faith-promise giving. Basically, the different schools of thought on faith promise agree that it involves making a promise to God to give Him a specific amount of money which you do not already have.

The term *faith-promise giving* is not found in the Scriptures, though the principle of asking God to provide something and dedicating it to him before it is received is found (1 Sam. 1:11f.). Hannah asked God for a son and promised to dedicate him to the Lord's work if God chose to answer her prayer. If God had not answered her prayer she would not have had anything to give. But God did answer her prayer and she kept her promise and gave her son, Samuel to God. God used him mightily as one of the great judges and prophets of Israel.

The principle Hannah used, of promising something to God if He will provide it, has been applied to the area of giving. The Bible doesn't contain any specific passage that admonishes us to do this, but it seems to be a valid application of a biblical principle that can be applied to finances. It provides an opportunity to allow God to supernaturally answer a specific prayer in a way which brings glory to Him.

Definition of Faith-Promise Giving

Faith-promise giving is asking God in faith for something specific, that you do not have, in order to give it entirely to His work. It is a level of giving which does not appear in your budget because it does not come from regular income. It a supernatural level of giving.

How Faith-Promise Giving Works

You pray for a specific amount that you would like to give to God's work. It could be a one-time gift or an amount which you would like to give monthly or weekly to help meet a need for God's work or His people.

Ask God to provide the means for you to give, from some source that you are not anticipating. When God provides the funds, give it entirely to Him. You cannot give it unless it comes in.

This is entirely a voluntary matter. No one should pressure you into participating in faith promise. You are no better or worse a Christian for participating or not.

You may desire to promise a portion of your income, above the tithe, to God's work. That is nice, but it must be done in accordance with God's order in finances. That is not faith promise. Faith promise is not promising God something you already have, then asking Him to make up the difference.

How Faith-Promise Giving Comes In

The answer to your faith promise can come in any way God chooses to provide it. He can do it dramatically or quite ordinarily. Sometimes the provision is so subtle you may not even recognize that God is actually the One providing in answer to your prayer.

Some such means may be a totally unexpected raise, an unexpected inheritance, gifts, increased profits, unexpected return on your investments, etc.

One person walked outside and, on her front step, found the exact amount she had asked God to provide for her faith promise.

I prayed for a specific amount one day, to give as a faith promise. The exact amount came unexpectedly in the mail the next week. It is exciting to see how God provides.

Where Should You Give?

Once you understand *what* you are to give, the next question to be answered is *where* should you give? Some people will agree with all the biblical principles up to this point. This is a touchy subject and one that is easily influenced by the ministry of which you are part. Every ministry seems to want you to give to them in particular.

God does have a design and order for giving. There are two basic principles in this area.

God's Plan does not allow any room for personal glory. Many people want others to know who helped meet a need. Though unintentionally, they are taking the glory away from God, because they, rather than God, become the source.

If you choose to give that way, you must remember to relish the feeling of satisfaction your giving brings you. That is the only reward you will receive from God for that giving (Matt. 6:1-4).

Though your flesh, and perhaps at times even your heart, would tell you to give this way, God has a different plan He wants you to follow. He wants you to give His way and find your joy in that. As you follow His plan, the needs will be met and an eternal reward will also await you.

God's plan is for His people to give through His assembly. God wants our giving directed through the local church, His assembly of believers, for a number of reasons.

Some people do not have the kind of relationship with their church to trust the funds to go where they should. A ministry that appeals for funds directly to individuals, may appeal to these type of Christians or to disgruntled or disillusioned Christians who would willingly give to something God is blessing, but do not want to give through their church.

If a church does not use its finances properly, don't violate God's plan by giving in some other way. Pray and work to see that the problem is corrected. If that doesn't work, then find another church. But don't forsake God's plan and program for giving.

In the Old Testament: through the Temple
(Mal. 3:10)

In the Old Testament God had his people bring their tithes and offerings to the temple – God's special place to meet with His people. It let the people know there was one place to give to the one true God and let them know that provision came from God. The temple became the storehouse, a sort of central dispensary for the funds for God's work.

The *tithes* which were brought there supported the priests, musicians, attendants, and others who worked in full-time service for God. It also helped support their families and others in need.

As the *tithes* helped support the work and people, the *offerings* helped build and maintain the physical structure at the temple.

In the New Testament: through the Local Church
(1 Cor. 16:2)

In the New Testament the local church assembled together as God's people. Often they did not have a building, but they were still His church as they gathered together to meet with God.

As in the Old Testament, the tithes and offerings were brought to God's meeting place. This time it was the local church. This let the people know again that there was one place to give to the one true God.

This local-church-centered giving also let the people know they could find provision from God. The church became somewhat of a storehouse, like the temple in the Old Testament, though it is never called that.

The tithes and offerings helped support the pastors and other Christian workers (1 Cor. 9:6-15). It helped the work of missions (Phil. 4:14-17). It helped meet physical needs of those within the local church (Acts 2:45; 6:1f.). It also helped support other ministries (1 Cor. 16:1).

Why Should We Give through the Church?

There are a number of reasons to direct your giving through the local church.

1. God chose the local church as His means today for showing His glory on Earth (Eph. 3:21).

2. God warns not to build on anything other than the local church (1 Cor. 3:10-15).

3. The local church is the only institution God has established other than the home and government. It alone has the promise that the gates of hell will not prevail against it (Matt. 16:18).

4. All ministries should be related to the local church and should be dependent on the local church for their support. This provides a level of accountability to all ministries, through the institution they are helping to grow (Eph. 4:11-12).

5. When giving is done through the local church, God receives all of the glory when needs are met. No personal glory or recognition is made, except in heaven (Matt. 6:1-4).

6. This allows all giving to be done with counsel before it is distributed (Acts 6:1-3).

7. God appointed deacons to distribute to the needs in the body (Acts 6:1-3).

8. Some needs or appeals for funds are not valid and the local church can help determine valid needs (Prov. 20:18).

What about Giving to Other Needs and Ministries?

If all giving should be done through the local church, how do you respond to needs presented by other ministries and God's people?

If you hear of a valid need, to which you believe God wants you to respond, designate your giving through your local church. The local church then serves as a clearinghouse, providing one last check to see if the need is valid. The need is then met by funds going through the local church and God gets the glory.

Before you give to help meet a need, be sure the following questions are answered about the ministry or person presenting the need.

Are They Local-Church Centered? All ministries should be local-church centered (Eph. 3:21; 1 Cor. 3:10-15; 1 Thess. 1:8).

There are basically two types of valid ministries:

Those in the Local Church (1 Cor. 12:28).   Based in individual churches, this ministry includes:

- *"apostles"* (those sent forth with an authoritative message). In the local church context this refers to outreach ministries to the local community (i.e., door-to-door evangelism, home Bible studies, Good News clubs, bus ministries, etc.).

- *"prophets"* (those who proclaim the Word primarily to God's people). In the local church context, those with preaching ministries (i.e., pastors, youth pastors, preachers in prison ministries, street preachers, etc.).

- *"teachers"* (those who explain God's Word and give practical application). Christian education ministries (i.e., Sunday School, children's ministries, youth programs, discipleship programs, etc.).

- *"miracles"* ministries which show forth the faith and life-changing power of God (i.e., prayer warriors, those who step out in faith to accomplish great things for God).

- *"gifts of healings"* (literally, those who repeatedly give therapy to heal from the inside out), could be counseling or health care ministries (i.e., counseling centers, homes for unwed mothers, teen hotlines, drug rehabilitation, etc.).

- *"helps"* various hands-on practical ministries (i.e., music ministries, food pantry, printing ministry, transportation ministries, etc.).

- *"governments"* (those who administer), administrative and organizational ministries (i.e., secretaries, trustees, directors of ministries, financial counselors, etc.).

- *"diversities of tongues"* (those who speak, expound or interpret in other languages), linguistical ministries (i.e., deaf interpreters, interpreters for various language groups, teachers for other language groups, cross-cultural ministries, etc.).

Those to the Local Church (Eph. 4:11). Ministries in various churches, either in your country or around the world, including:

- *"apostles"* (those sent forth with a message), those involved in ministries which lead to planting churches (i.e., church-planters, missionaries, Bible translators, international radio ministries, etc.).

- *"prophets"* (those who proclaim the Word primarily to God's people), revival-type ministries (i.e., Bible conferences, revivalists, seminar ministries, some music ministries, etc.).

- *"evangelists"* (those who proclaim the Gospel to the lost), evangelistic ministries (i.e., evangelists, outreach ministries, some music ministries, etc.).

- *"pastors"* (those who pasture the sheep) pastoral ministries (i.e., pastors, counseling ministries, etc.).

- *"teachers"* teaching ministries (i.e., Bible institutes and colleges, Bible teachers, teaching ministries, etc.).

God's Word says all of the above are valid ministries and therefore warrant the support of His people.

There are times when ministries are more effective working as a team or with other believers as they minister to the local church. Such organizations are missionary, revival, evangelistic, pastoral or teaching and exist to strengthen the local church. Therefore, they should receive their support from the local church. Does your church support the broad range of ministries God's Word says He has established?

Individual giving to these various ministries would be best channeled through the local church. Any designated giving should go entirely to the specified ministry. If the church feels there is a reason the funds should not go to that particular ministry, the church should explain this to the individual who gave the designated gift and return the funds.

A *"no"* answer to any of these questions should be a sufficient reason not to send funds to a ministry.

Are They Doctrinally Sound? Unless a ministry is true to the teaching of the inspired, infallible, inerrant Word of God, they should not receive support from God's people (Rom. 16:17).

Does God Receive the Glory through This Ministry? There will always be people who are blessed by a ministry or by a man, and will then speak highly of them, but that does not mean God is receiving the glory.

There are many ministries where man or ministry takes more glory than God. That is wrong. Often those types of ministries are named after men (John 7:18; 2 Cor. 10:17; Gal. 6:14).

What Is the Fruit of Their Ministry? All Christians and ministries will be judged on the basis of their fruit which remains, the stability and long-lasting effects of their ministry (Matt. 7:15-23; John 15:1-8; 1 Cor. 3:13-15).

There is much work done today for Christ or in the name of Christ, which will not remain.

Answer the following questions to determine the fruit of a ministry:

- *Are there lasting, life-transforming results in the lives of people who have been affected by this ministry?*
- *Are people being genuinely saved though this ministry?*
- *Is the emphasis on salvation and spiritual growth or only on the sensational and spectacular?*
- *Are projects which are started, brought to completion?*
- *Do the attempted outreaches continue?*
- *Is the local church strengthened by this ministry?*
- *Does this ministry have perpetuity (a means for carrying on past the present individuals involved)?*

Do They Exhibit Wise Stewardship? God said we are *stewards* and are *required* to be faithful (1 Cor. 4:1-2). A ministry must adhere to the biblical principles of stewardship. Anything less would be sin.

Any ministry that does not follow God's principles of finances should not be supported, no matter how emotional an appeal they make or no matter how great the need may seem.

Answer the following questions to help you determine the faithfulness of a ministry to God's principles of finances:

- *Do they adhere to the principle of "owe no man anything" and trust God to provide or do they borrow money for their ministry?*

- *Do they violate biblical principles and spend what they do not have, in anticipation of future income?*

- *Do they operate on a financial system using a budget and a means of accounting to their supporters?*

- *Are they careful with funds and materials or are they wasteful or extravagant?*

Is Their Present Need Valid? Many appeals for funds from ministries are valid, but many are not. It is important to determine if the request is for a valid need.

- *Perhaps there is a genuine need.*

- *Perhaps there has been poor stewardship which created the need.*

- *Perhaps the ministry is trying to do something God does not want them to do.*

- *Perhaps there is a need which no one else is meeting and God wants them to meet.*

- *Perhaps some other ministry is meeting this need and this is needless duplication.*

Some Practical Thoughts about Giving

Hopefully the following pointers will help you as you seek to apply God's principles.

Give to God, Not for a Tax Deduction. The current tax laws in the United States allow you to take some deductions for donations made to God's work. You should claim any such deductions you are entitled to, but don't let that be your motivation for giving. One day those deductions may no longer be there.

Be aware of changes in the tax law that affect the status of your deductions so you get the maximum benefit from the law and claim your deductions properly. Remember the following tax related principles, which are subject to change:

• *If you make out a check to an individual missionary, rather than their ministry, it is not tax deductible.*

• *If you receive a gift in return for your giving, the retail value of the gift must be deducted from the amount of the donation, when you claim your deductions.*

• *Services rendered to a ministry are deductible, if rendering those services is your occupation.*

There Are Other Ways to Give Besides Giving Money. Giving money is not the only way to give to a ministry. There are various ways you can give to help a ministry.

• *You can give clothing.* Gifts of used clothing in good condition or new clothing is appreciated by many ministries.

• *You can give food.* A food closet could be set up at your church where people bring nonperishable goods each week to stockpile for visiting missionaries, evangelists, and for meeting needs within the local church or community.

• *You can make things to give.* Some people make clothing, quilts, crafts, computer systems, etc. to give to God's work. I met a man who builds airplanes and gives a certain number each year to God's work.

• *You can give new or used equipment.* Lots of people have equipment around their home that they rarely use, but that could be used extensively in God's work (i.e., cameras, camcorders, slide projectors, computers, heaters, fans, typewriters, tents, trailers, etc.).

• *You can give your time.* Many people have time and talents that could greatly help God's work. Perhaps you could volunteer some time each month or week. Perhaps you could take some vacation time and help God's work. Whatever your talent, it can be used somewhere in God's work.

- *You can remember birthdays, holidays and special days for those in Christian service.* What joy you can bring by writing a letter or sending a card or little gift. You will never know what an encouragement that is to people.

- *Brainstorm with others and come up with more ideas for giving.*

Don't Let Others Make You Feel Guilty about Giving.

Some people may try to make you feel guilty about the way you give. You should not feel guilty if you are following the biblical principles of finances.

Some people will tell you to give until it hurts. The Bible doesn't say that. The Bible says give cheerfully. It is a joy to give. If it hurts someone to give, they are not giving God's way.

Some will make great emotional appeals to make you feel guilty so you will give. Give according to God's principles, not because someone can make you cry. There are some needs which may not make you cry, but are more valid than the ones which do.

One pastor who is no longer in the ministry used to tell his congregation that if they loved God they would put something in the offering plate every time it was passed. He used false guilt to motivate those people to give. They passed the plate for the general offering both in Sunday School and in the morning service and in the evening service and expected each person to give something every time.

I asked him how people were supposed to be able to earn something between Sunday School and morning service to give, or for that matter how were they supposed to earn something Sunday afternoon to give on Sunday evening?

He said that what he did, was divide his tithe between the offering in Sunday School, the Sunday morning service, the Sunday evening service and midweek Service. He never told the people that.

Guilt or shame is not a proper motivation for giving.

Write Your Tithe Check as Soon as Possible. Don't hold on to your tithe. Give it as soon as possible. Things will happen to test your faithfulness.

Establish a Giving Reserve Fund. If you can establish a Giving Reserve Fund in which you deposit a regular amount, you will have greater flexibility to use in giving to needs and may be able to make a more significant impact in helping meet a larger need. Be careful that you don't hoard this.

Give Some Time in Prayer. Although giving to meet a need is important, don't forget the importance of praying that God will supply the need for that ministry. Consider giving time in prayer for various ministries.

A Final Thought about Giving

Biblical giving is a grace in which God wants you to abound. He does not force you to give. After you give God the tithe in honor of His lordship, the rest is a grace you may choose to participate in. It is something He wants you to cheerfully take part in, with the abundance He so freely gives you (2 Cor. 9:7).

There are many who will never know the joy of the biblical principles of finances until they have participated in the grace of giving. There are others who will never know the measure of abundance God desires to bestow on them, because they would only use it selfishly on themselves. The choice is yours.

"And God is able to make all Grace abound toward you; that ye, always having all sufficiency in all things, may abound to every good work" (2 Cor. 9:8).

For Review and Reflection...

1. What are the different types of giving for the believer today?

2. What is faith-promise giving?

3. What are the two basic principles to remember regarding giving?

4. Why should you give through the local church?

5. What are some valid types of ministries to which you may give?

6. What questions should you ask before you give to a ministry?

7. What are some practical tips regarding giving that you can apply to your situation?

Chapter Eight
DETERMINING GOD'S DIRECTION IN FINANCES

Every day of your life, numerous situations come your way, which require some type of decision. Sometimes after making so many decisions, you make decisions without even thinking much about them. Other times you find yourself pondering over the choices before you as you carefully and intentionally seek to make the right decision.

Some decisions are obviously important, like choosing a mate, finding a job or deciding if you should relocate. Although some decisions may not seem as important as others, all decisions are important. The decisions you make today will affect your tomorrow.

Some decisions may seem very minor at the time, like deciding what you should eat for lunch today or what you should wear tonight. Yet, what you eat is important because it affects your health and what you wear is important because it protects your body and communicates a message to others. All of your decisions are important.

Wouldn't it be great if you could talk to someone who knew what affect your decisions would have before you made them? Someone with that kind of perspective could provide you with some very valuable direction and guidelines to help you to make the best decisions.

There is someone like that who is willing and able to help you make each decision in your life. He is the Alpha, the Omega, the beginning and the end (Rev. 1:8), the One to whom yesterday, today, and tomorrow are a present reality (Ps. 90:4; Heb. 13:8). He is the Lord Jesus Christ. Through prayer, godly counsel, and seeking His will through His Word, He will give you the wisdom you need to make the right decisions.

The Word of God contains many principles that serve as guidelines to help you make the right decisions and to determine God's direction for your life. To make the best decisions in life you need to apply God's principles in the decision-making process.

The biblical principles of finances not only help you experience the freedom of debt-free living and know the joy of abundant giving, but they provide you with guidelines and mileposts to help you gain God's perspective as you face important decisions in your life. Understanding the biblical principles of finances will help you to recognize how God is leading you as you see changes in your financial situation.

You do not need to know the biblical principles of finances to know when your financial situation has changed significantly (Mal. 3:7-12). Changes in your financial situation have a way of getting your attention. These changes are one method God uses to get your attention so He can provide direction in your life. Understanding His principles will help you see that direction more clearly and make the right decisions.

Review Some of the Biblical Principles of Finances

The following basic biblical principles of finances serve as guidelines to help you determine God's direction in your life.

You Are a Steward
(1 Cor. 4:1-2)

As a steward you are a manager of what God has entrusted to you. Everything you have belongs to God. Acknowledge His ownership and allow Him to direct you in managing His estate. He will give you the wisdom and grace you need as you attempt to be a faithful steward.

In Whatever You Do, God Should Get the Glory
(1 Cor. 6:20)

This is especially true of the way you handle your finances. In everything you do, seek to give God the glory.

There are some things which in and of themselves may not be bad, but do not glorify God. Avoid doing those things. Let the financial decisions you make bring glory to God.

God Has an Order in Finances That He Expects You to Follow
(1 Cor. 14:40)

A crucial principle to remember is to follow God's order in finances. Many opportunities that arise would violate His order. Experience the joy that comes with following God's order in finances: Tithe -> Taxes -> Family Needs -> Debt Repayment -> then Abundance.

God Has Promised to Meet Your Needs
(Matt. 6:33)

God has promised to meet all your needs. If your needs do not seem to be met, you must ask yourself why that situation exists. Your spiritual needs are always greater than your physical needs. Sometimes God allows physical discomfort to strengthen you spiritually.

Another very important aspect of this principle is to learn to distinguish between your *needs* and *wants*. We often want more than we need and must know the difference between the two.

God Expects You to Pray for Your Needs Daily
(Matt. 6:11)

Don't presume upon God, pray for your needs. Even though He has promised to provide, He told us to pray.

Remember He is your source, not your job, not your wisdom, not your abilities. He provides you a job. He then gives you the strength and ability to do it. Lift your job up in prayer to the Lord.

Don't worry about His provision. Things may look bleak at times but worrying never changes your financial situation for the better.

God Does Not Want You to Go in Debt
(Rom. 13:8)

Live the principle of *"owe no man anything."* Going in debt is not something God wants you to do. If you find yourself on that path, remember, the Bible teaches that debt indicates a lack of God's blessing. Those in debt in the Bible were under the chastising hand of God.

God Does Not Want You to Presume upon Tomorrow
(Prov. 27:1)

Don't forget, God wants you to follow the *"ant principle"* and begin to prepare today for tomorrow. He wants you prepared for retirement and to have an inheritance to leave for your children and grandchildren. Don't spend tomorrow's money, today.

God Is Still God
(Jer. 33:3)

God is still in control; nothing takes Him by surprise. He doesn't make any mistakes with you. He works all things together for good (Rom. 8:28). That doesn't mean everything that happens in your life *is* good. It means He makes it *work together* for your good.

Be in prayer and allow Him to work in and through you. Let His love and power shine through. Allow Him to be God in your life.

God Blesses Obedience
(2 Cor. 9:6-8)

God blesses obedience. Seek to apply His principles in your life so you can reflect His grace and blessing. As you become aware of a biblical principle, apply it and allow God to work. He wants to bless you and He wants you in the place of blessing so you can be a channel through which he can pass His blessings along to others.

God Loves You So Much That He Will Correct You
If You Violate His Principles
(Prov. 3:3-12)

If you violate any of God's principles, He knows it will hurt you. He loves you so much that if you do violate His principles, He will correct you, so you can be restored to the place of blessing.

Determining God's Direction in Your Life
and Your Family's Life

There are various situations where you can apply the biblical principles of finances as guidelines to help you make the right decisions and to determine God's direction.

Determining Your Life Work

As you decide what occupation you should pursue or if you are considering a change in your occupation, use the following biblical principles of finances as guidelines.

God Expects You to Work (Mark 13:34-37; 2 Thess. 3:10). Some people wrongly believe the reason they get a job is so they can pay the bills and one day retire so they don't have to work any more.

Some people view paradise as a place where they don't have to work. They think it would be a blessing if they didn't have to work. That is a real misunderstanding. God made us in such a way that we need to work and need to be productive to find fulfillment. Even in paradise Adam had a job.

If you are physically able, God expects you to work. Some people have the attitude that the world owes them a living and want to get by with the least amount of effort as is possible. That is wrong. No one owes anyone a living. God wants you to pray and work for what you have. If you can work and you don't, then He says you shouldn't eat.

Although children should be cared for by their parents, as they are growing up, when they are able to work they should not be living off their parents or off of society.

Encourage the work ethic as your children grow up. It is interesting to note how little children like to help, even though sometimes their help can be more of a hindrance. That desire to help is part of their God-given need to be productive. Some parents make a mistake when they don't figure out a way for their children to help in a way they can feel productive. It is important to teach children how to work, then to reward those efforts.

Though work requires effort and though at times is hard, it is rewarding to work. Children need to learn that at an early age. They need to feel the reward of accomplishing something. One very serious mistake some parents make is to make work a punishment. No wonder so many children don't want to work when they grow up. Work should never be a punishment. It should be a reward.

Situations sometimes arise that affect someone's ability to work. In those cases public insurance and welfare are valid vehicles to help people through hardships. It is actually the job of the church to help take care of the needy, the widow, and the ones who can't stand on their own two feet. But if the church doesn't meet those needs, it is valid to utilize the services the state offers.

God's Word does not condone a welfare society that fosters a segment of society which does not work when they can. As you seek God's direction, don't look for hand-outs or the easy road. Be willing to carry your share of the load, to work hard, and put good effort into what you believe God would have you do.

The only thing that you should get free is salvation – which cost God the life of His Only Son to give to you.

God Expects Your Work to Glorify Him (Col. 3:17, 24). You can and should glorify God through your work. You do not have to be in professional full-time Christian service to glorify God with your job. If God has called you into some other line of work, you can glorify Him there too. Some jobs would be hard to glorify God with. Can you think of some?

Some jobs you could accept are not wrong in and of themselves, but their requirements such as the schedule they demand, may be detrimental to your health, your family life or your spiritual life. Such constraints could make it difficult for you to glorify God in that situation.

God has given you abilities and desires which will enable you to do a job that brings both fulfillment in your life and glory to Him at the same time.

As you consider God's direction in your life, ask yourself, Would this job and its associated responsibilities allow me to bring the most glory to God?

God Expects You to Find Work to Meet the Needs of Your Family (1 Tim. 5:8). It is important to work and to glorify God in your work, but it is also important that your work brings in enough income to support your family.

Your work can be recreation but often your recreation does not make good work. Some people have left good jobs to do something they enjoy as a hobby only to find out it does not bring in sufficient income. That in turn creates stress and hardship on the family.

Although God is your source, He expects you to work in such a way that it helps to meet the needs of your family.

It is interesting to note how God gave the husband in the family the title *"father"* – one of God's names. God gave fathers one of His names to remind us of the awesome responsibility they have to provide for their families as He provides for His people. When fathers do not help provide for their families, it makes it hard for their families to understand how God the Father provides for them. Providing the needs for their families does not only mean physical needs, but emotional and spiritual needs.

As you seek God's direction in your life, always be sure you are in a place that will help you meet the needs of your family.

You Should Have a Secure Job before You Get Married (Prov. 24:27). This is perhaps one of the most ignored biblical principles in some societies. God says it is best for you to be sure you know what you are doing with your life, prepare for that task and begin to undertake it, before you get married.

Desire and impatience often cloud reason and lead to premature marriages. It is possible with God's help to overcome the obstacles you will encounter if you don't heed this principle, but that is not God's ideal.

As societies move away from this standard, more and more

marriages do not survive the storms of life they encounter, storms which God did not intend for them to face.

This does not mean you have to be at your job for years, but it does imply a stability should be established before marriage. It also does not mean God will not move you or change your job after you are married. This principle protects the wife and children by being sure the husband has a job which can meet their needs before a family is established.

As you seek God's direction in your life, have you or your potential mate established yourselves in your life work? Be sure you have done this before you enter into that lifetime commitment. Some think the trials they share will bring them closer together, and in some ways they are right, but trials also drive many apart before they are ready to handle them. Trust God and apply this principle.

God Expects You to Have Some Type of Ministry (Rom. 12:1-8). God has equipped you to serve Him. Be sure that you have some type of ministry wherever you are. Some people say their ministry is to their family, that is true. Yet that is only one aspect of your ministry. God has given you a gift and abilities He wants you to use to minister to the body of Christ.

Some people make the mistake of saying they will work more at their jobs and give now, then serve later. Don't wait until tomorrow to serve God (John 4:35). He wants you to serve Him now.

As you seek God's direction in your life be sure you have a ministry where you can use your gift to serve Him.

Work and Money Will Try to Take Priority in Your Life (Matt. 6:19-24). Money wants you to serve it instead of God. Financial pressures or financial opportunities will come to try to draw you away from God. Remember, Satan offered Jesus riches and the kingdoms of this world if He would turn aside from the task before Him (Luke 4:5-8). If He tempted the Lord that way don't you think he'll do as much with you?

The love of money has turned many people away from serving God (1 Tim. 6:10). Many times they are turned aside by financial opportunities which in themselves are not wrong, but which lead them astray down the road. Be prayerful and careful.

As you seek God's direction in your life realize that some opportunities will not always be the right thing to follow. Carefully consider each promotion, each transfer, each opportunity, in light of biblical principles.

Regarding Choosing a Place to Live

Everyone needs a place to live. As you look around the world you will find believers living in all types of situations. Some live in houses, some live in tents, some live in houseboats. Apply God's principles as you seek the place in which God would have you live.

God Never Promised That You Will Own Your Own House (Matt. 8:20). God promised that He will take care of His children but He never promised that Christians would own their own houses. He may allow you to own a house, but your spirituality, physical well-being, and happiness do not depend on that. There are many good Christians who have never owned their own houses.

There is a difference between a house and a home. There is a good measure of truth in the old saying, "Home is where the heart is." You do not need to own your house to have a good home.

Don't Violate God's Principles to Secure a House. If the door for home ownership opens for you, be sure you do not violate any biblical principles to walk through it. Some people put so much effort into securing a home they neglect some other area of their life, which in turn hurts them spiritually. Be sure you adhere to all of God's principles as you consider home ownership.

Be Sure Your Work Is Established before You Purchase a House (Prov. 24:37). You should be sure of what you are doing with your life before you buy a house. Acquiring a house is a big commitment and should not be undertaken lightly. It is not a pleasant thing to have your home taken away from you because you cannot maintain it any longer.

Though a house can be a good investment, sometimes it isn't. If you do not have your life's work established you may want to consider some other type of investment.

There is a tremendous financial commitment necessary to secure a home. That burden could be eased by a return to the biblical principle of parents and grandparents taking an active role in helping to secure housing. Housing was part of the inheritance left to the children in the Bible (Prov. 19:14; 13:22). Land and a home was something that was passed on through the generations and helped provide stability. This was not cosigning for an irresponsible son, but helping a son who had shown himself responsible. The son did not become engaged until he could provide for a family. Then his parents and grandparents helped him secure housing and he was married.

What are you doing to prepare for helping your children and grandchildren secure housing?

Don't Move to Egypt, Sodom or Moab (spiritually speaking). There are some situations and places where attractive housing will be available but which may be harmful to you spiritually.

Egypt and Moab were places of plenty when times were hard in the promised land, but it was not where God wanted His people. It resulted in deceit with Abraham, bondage for Jacob and his descendants, and a loss of almost everything for Naomi. When things are hard, don't leave where God led you to go where things look better.

Sodom was a prosperous place and appealed to Lot, but he lost his family through the influence of the Sodomites. Beware of the lure of prosperity. It may stuff your pocketbook but destroy you and your family spiritually.

Always Consider the Spiritual Consequences of a Move. Every decision we make has some type of spiritual consequence, especially the decision to move your place of residence.

Seek God's will and godly counsel before moving. What are the spiritual benefits and liabilities of such a move? Is there a good church in the area? Is there opportunity for ministry? What spiritual effects could moving or not moving have on your family?

Regarding Acquiring Wants and Needs

God promised to provide your needs. He also wants to give you your desires. There are some biblical principles to keep in mind regarding the acquisition of our needs and wants.

It is Easy to Violate God's Principles in This Area (Eph. 5:18). You must remember the application of biblical principles is a spiritual matter. If you do not depend on the Holy Spirit, you may easily violate one of the principles, no matter how sincere you are.

Pray about ALL Financial Needs and Expenditures (1 Thess 5:17). If we are to pray without ceasing and if God is interested in every aspect of our lives, then we ought to pray about all our financial needs and expenditures.

It is a blessing to ask God for wisdom regarding each expenditure (James 1:5). This includes Him in even the smallest details of your life and is something He honors.

As I am on the road, I pray about where to eat lunch, what to buy, what motel to stay in, etc. There is a special fellowship in discussing these things with God.

One time I helped a person replace a roof on their house. Unexpectedly they gave me $300. The same day someone offered me a tremendous deal on a set of speakers which would have been a real help to my music ministry. They wanted $300 for the pair of speakers. I had the exact amount of money and could have really used the speakers. Buying the speakers seemed the thing to do. When I prayed about it, the Lord impressed upon me that I had been praying for other needs and the $300 was provided to meet those needs. I wanted the speakers and could use them, but God provided the money in answer to another prayer.

Pray as you go grocery shopping, pray as you buy your clothing, pray regarding your bills, pray before you make an investment. Pray and allow God to give you the wisdom or provision you need. If you feel awkward praying about a financial expenditure perhaps you should not spend it.

A Sale Does Not Mean that God Wants You to Buy Something. If you have to buy something, it is always a blessing to find it on sale and save money. However, just because something is on sale does not mean it is a good buy nor does it mean it is something God wants you to have.

A person once told me, if you *need* an item and an item is on sale when you have the money, then you should buy it. That advice needs one more ingredient. If the above is true, only buy the item if you have prayed for it and if God impresses upon you that you should buy it.

There was a time I prayed for a new pair of shoes. The pair I had were resoled but were wearing out and needed to be replaced. One day someone walked up to me and gave me $60 and said to use it to buy a pair of shoes. I began praying for wisdom to know which pair to buy. There was a sale at a shoe store in town so I went to see if they had a pair which would work for me. The store had an acceptable pair on sale and had the right size. It would have seemed the thing to do to buy that pair of shoes, but God impressed upon my heart not to do that. To me that was strange. I needed the shoes, the shoes were on sale, and I had the money. I left the shoe store perplexed but knowing I was doing the right thing.

One week later I was driving downtown and saw a sale sign in an expensive shoe shop. I didn't plan to stop because I figured that even on sale I couldn't afford a pair of shoes in that store. Then I saw a person I knew standing in the store with a few pairs of shoes in her hands. I was somewhat familiar with her financial situation and knew there was no way she could normally afford one pair of shoes in that store, much less the few pairs she was holding. I parked my car and went inside. To my surprise I found out the store was going out of business and was clearing out all its shoes for $5 per pair for adult shoes and $5 for two pairs of children's shoes.

I found two pairs of shoes that fit me and paid just $10 for them. I then went home and got my wife, four children, and two of the neighbors children who needed shoes and was able to buy each person two pairs of shoes. Instead of getting one pair of shoes for myself for $60 I was able to buy two pairs of nice shoes for each of the eight people. Prayer and patience are very important in acquiring your wants and needs.

Learn to Resist Salespeople (Prov. 20:14; 11:14). A salesperson's job is to make a sale, not to give you a great deal or to watch out for your best interests. You must learn to resist salespeople.

A whole variety of salespeople are waiting to get your money. Some are called salespeople; others are go by different names. Can you think of some obvious and not so obvious salesmen? Obvious ones are the vacuum cleaner salesperson, the used car salesperson, and the Avon lady. Some nonobvious salespeople are the insurance agent, the mortgage broker, and the banker. Each of them have a service that comes with a price tag, though you may not see it dangling in front of you.

A salesperson may appear to give you good advice, but they always seem to recommend their product or their investment. Get additional counsel before making any reasonable size expenditure.

God Expects You to Use Wisdom in Your Purchases (James 1:5). Apply wisdom in order to be a good steward as you make purchases. Sometimes a store brand is as good as the more expensive name brand. Sometimes it isn't. Sometimes an item on sale in one store may be less expensive at the regular price in another store.

A good warranty can increase the value of some purchases. Some companies guarantee their products, no questions asked. Some say that but no questions are asked because you can never find the company again to ask it the questions.

Technology is one area which is changing so much that it is very important to seek advice and wisdom when buying any equipment with electronic components.

It takes practice to learn to shop wisely.

Apply the Proverbs 6:6-8, Ant Principle. The ant prepares in the summer for the coming hard months of winter. You must learn to apply this principle to your finances.

Begin to set aside now for expenditures you know you are going to have in the future. Don't wait until you absolutely have to have an item before you start saving for it.

Can you think of items you are going to need to purchase or replace in the next few months? What about in the next year or three years? What are you doing to prepare for that expense you know you are going to have.

If you applied this principle to car purchases you would save hundreds and hundreds of dollars. You would make a car payment to yourself, paying cash for your next car and then make payments to yourself again. You do twice as good than if you went out and financed a car. Not only would you earn interest on the money set aside, you wouldn't pay interest to someone else.

Let God Provide (Phil 4:19). Too often we rush out to pay for what we should wait and pray for. Let God provide an answer to your prayers. Undertake all the efforts of wise stewardship and setting aside, then pray and let God provide His way. Sometimes God has us prepare, but intervenes with His provision. Too many of us have never tasted the manna from heaven because we are content to eat from our own little pot.

Regarding Bills That Are Due

Paying bills is one of those aspects of life many of us would gladly do without. As you face the routine of regular bills and larger bills that come due periodically, you need to keep in mind the following principles.

God Expects You to Budget ahead for Bills (Prov. 6:6-8).

If you set aside something each pay period, you will have the funds in place when a bill comes due. Coming up with the entire sum when a bill is due to is too difficult. This is especially true with larger payments like taxes, insurance, and purchasing a vehicle.

Even if you set aside only a little at a time, that little begins to accumulate and helps lighten the pressure when a bill comes due.

Often God provides us with a little more than we need, not to spend but to prepare us in advance for coming expenses. Don't spend funds which God has provided for approaching expenditures.

God May Not Provide the Funds Until the Day the Bill Is Due, to Test Your Faith (Matt. 6:25-34). God can and will meet all your needs. Though He wants you to save ahead for coming expenditures, sometimes that will not be possible. There may be times when a bill is due tomorrow and there isn't any money to pay the bill today. Worrying about where the finances will come from won't do any good. Instead you need to pray (Phil 4:6). God does not need to provide the money today if the bill is not due till tomorrow. Often He does provide in advance to help us develop the principles of stewardship, but sometimes He waits until the last minute to provide, to strengthen our faith.

If a Bill Is Due and the Funds are Not There to Pay, Ask Yourself the Following Questions:

- *Is it a valid bill?* Is the bill one you should have incurred? Perhaps it is for something you should not have acquired. Perhaps you are living outside of your means.

- *Is there unconfessed sin in your life?* If you have known sin in your life (Ps. 66:18), God turns off the answers to your prayers and often turns off His supply line to get your attention. Deal with the sin if it is there – confess it and forsake it.

- *Did you misspend the funds?* Often God provides the funds in advance, sometimes only a little at a time, but we misspend them. Have you bought something you shouldn't have or did you use the funds on something else?

• *Is God directing you toward a change?* If you have dealt with the other questions satisfactorily then perhaps the provision is not there so God can get your attention in order to redirect you. Do some serious soul-searching. Not paying your bills is a bad testimony and brings too much pressure on you and your family.

Seek the Lord's direction and He will show you what to do if you are willing to follow what He shows you to do (James 1:5-8).

As you apply the biblical principles of finances they will bring a new freedom and victory in your life and a real peace in knowing God is pleased with the way you are handling what He has entrusted to you.

For Review and Reflection...

1. How would knowing the biblical principles of finances help you as you face various decisions in life?

2. What are some of the basic biblical principles of finances you should remember as you seek God's direction in your life?

3. What are some principles to keep in mind when determining your life work?

4. What are some principles to keep in mind regarding choosing a place to live?

5. What are some principles to keep in mind regarding acquiring wants and needs?

6. What are some principles to keep in mind regarding bills that are due?

7. What are the questions you should ask yourself if a bill is due but you do not have the funds for it?

Appendix One
SIMPLE BASIC SAVINGS PLAN FOR THE BEGINNER

The following plan is a simple way to get on the path to saving and investing your money.

STEP 1 – Open a **N.O.W. Account.** Use this account to operate your budget. Deposit the savings portion of your budget in this account until it reaches $500-$1,000, whichever balance is required to earn free checking, interest, and no service charges.

STEP 2 – Deposit savings over the $500-$1,000 from the N.O.W. Account into a **Savings Account,** if it offers a higher rate of return.

STEP 3 – Transfer the interest earned on the N.O.W. Account to the Savings Account, where it will earn more interest each month.

STEP 4 – When the Savings Account has $1,000 in it, open a **Money Market Account.** This will provide a higher rate of interest and still provide accessibility to your funds.

STEP 5 – Continue to deposit savings into the Money Market until you have the equivalent of 3 to 6 months take-home salary in it. This becomes your **Emergency Fund.**

STEP 6 – Continue to deposit savings into the Money Market. When you have enough funds in excess of your Emergency Fund figure, open a **Mutual Fund, Money Market Mutual Fund,** or **Growth Fund** for Investment. Consider buying some **Savings Bonds** and **Certificates of Deposit.**

STEP 7 – Open an **I.R.A.** (Individual Retirement Fund) now that you have some experience in the investment world. Don't use tax-exempt funds. Remember that an I.R.A. is tax-deferred. If you are self-employed you should open an I.R.A. or Keough earlier with the retirement portion of your budget.

Appendix Two
WHAT TYPE OF LIFE INSURANCE IS BEST?

There are many different types of life insurance. The market is constantly changing. Prayerfully and carefully seek advice before buying life insurance.

What Is Life Insurance?

Life insurance is a pool of money into which you pay, anticipating that you will die before you save enough money to meet your family's needs. It is a means of providing protection in case the expected happens *before* you expect it to.

You pay a premium for a certain amount of insurance. The amount of insurance you buy is called the *Face Value.* If you buy a $100,000 policy, $100,000 is the face value. It doesn't matter how long you pay your premiums, if you keep your payments up to date, when you die, your survivors will receive the face value of your policy.

The amount of your policy should be the buffer to provide that which your investments will not provide for your family.

What Is Cash Value Life Insurance?

A cash value policy goes by different names, but is any life insurance policy which includes a forced savings plan.

The insured pays a constant premium until death or retirement, whichever comes first. If the insured dies, the face value of the policy is paid to the *beneficiaries* (designated survivors). The savings portion is forfeited under many policies, but is paid to the survivors under some.

If the insured lives to retirement, monthly payments are made to the insured from the investment portion of the policy, known as the *cash value*, until the day of his or her death. Or the insured has the option to receive the cash value in one lump sum payment when the retirement date of the policy is reached.

The interest rates on some cash value life insurance policies may appear competitive with market rates, but those rates are usually not guaranteed. Almost without exception, a much lower rate of return is guaranteed for your money. Some accept this type of policy because they need the discipline of being forced to save.

This type of policy also offers you the option to borrow from your cash value at a low interest rate. The drawback of that is you are still paying someone else for borrowing your own money. It is not yours to freely use.

What Is Term Life Insurance?

Term life insurance is pure insurance. It is an insurance policy for a fixed period of time, with a constant amount of coverage. The policy can often be renewed for another term at a higher premium.

If the insured dies, the *face value* of the policy is paid to the beneficiaries. At the end of the term there isn't any cash value.

Term policies often cost considerably less than *cash value policies* because of the absence of the savings portion in the premium.

If you want cash value, buy a term policy and invest the difference between what you would pay for a cash value policy. You then have the full use of your savings portion. You don't need to pay someone else interest to use it and your family gets both the face value of your term policy and the full amount of your savings on your death.

There are various types of term insurance:

Decreasing Term. Under these policies, the insured pays a fixed premium throughout the policy, with the amount of coverage decreasing each year. This is often the type of insurance the banks require for a mortgage holder. Less insurance is needed each year as the principal on the mortgage is reduced.

Level Term. A specific amount of coverage is secured for a specific term (5, 10, 15, 20 years) with a constant payment. Renewable policies for additional terms are usually available at a higher premium.

Annual Renewable Term. A year-to-year policy where the coverage stays the same and the premium gets larger. You usually have the option of taking out less coverage the next year for somewhat near the same premium.

Cash Value vs. Term Life Insurance

CASH VALUE POLICY   TERM POLICY
$100,000 $100,000

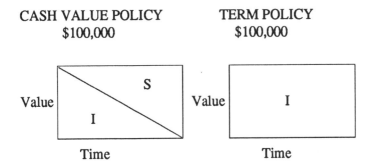

Notice the following observations based on the two charts that compare cash value and term life insurance.

1. Half way through the cash value policy you are paying more of your premium for your cash value portion.

2. Compare the difference in policies for a male age 34 with $100,000 coverage:

	A Very Good Cash Value Policy	An Average 15 -Year Level Term Policy w/ Renewable Option
Premium	$ 713 per year 486 next 5 years 780 next 5 years 1,165 next 5 years	$180 per year (first 15 years)
Total Premiums	x 31 years	1,875 last year
till Age 65	$ 22,103 TOTAL	$ 16,730 TOTAL

	Cash Value Policy	15-Year Level Term Policy *Investing the Premium Difference*
	[Both based on the estimated 8.5% return stated in the cash value policy]	
Cash Value after 5 years	$ 2,349	$ 3,451
10 years	7,943	8,702
15 years	14,370	16,688
20 years	23,433	26,854
26 years	39,835	43,456
At Age 65	$ 60,499	$ 62,400

- The term policy premiums costs less for the first 20 years, then cost more than the cash value policy for the remainder of the policy, though the total premium payments are lower.
- The term policy produces 47% more income than the cash value policy at the end of 5 years. By 10 years it drops to 10% and by Age 65 to a 3% lead.
- The savings portion of cash value policy can be borrowed at a specific rate of interest. The savings set aside separately from the term policy are available without penalties.
- Remember the interest rates are not guaranteed. The cash value policy states it guarantees a 4.5% return, but anticipates an 8.5% return. You can usually get a better rate on your own savings plan.
- At the same rate of return, the term policy slightly hedges out the cash value policy if the same level of insurance is maintained.
- If you reduce the amount of term insurance as your savings increase, rather than renew for the same amount of coverage, you will have more to invest and you will outperform the cash value policy by an even greater margin.
3. It is often better to buy annual renewable term or level term than it is to buy a cash value policy, then invest the difference for a better rate of return. When it comes time to renew your term policy, reduce your coverage proportionately to the increase in your savings. You will also find that your insurance needs decrease over the years. Reevaluate your insurance needs from time to time. Shop around for the best rates for policies.

Appendix Three
TYPES OF INVESTMENTS

Become familiar with the various types of investments available to you so you can make the best choice in the stewardship of the funds with which God has entrusted you.

This section provides only a brief overview of some common investment vehicles. New types of investments are being developed almost monthly and existing ones undergo various changes and modifications. As the economy changes so does the profitability and safety of some of these investments.

Many financial counselors recommend a *diversified portfolio of investments*. What that means is, they recommend that you place what you have to invest in a variety of investments. The investments you hold are referred to as your *portfolio*.

Always seek God's wisdom and godly counsel before making any investment.

NOTE: The figures stated for minimum investment and rate of return vary from institution to institution and may fluctuate with changes in the economy.

Short-Term Investments

These are financial investments you make which you may need to withdraw within 30 days to one year. These investments should be liquid (readily accessible if you need the cash).

Passbook or Statement Savings. A traditional way to start a savings account. Usually opened at a local Savings Bank. Not a good account to keep much of your savings in because of its low return.

Minimum Investment: Some have a minimum of $50-100.

Yield: About 5.5% compounded monthly or quarterly, but varies. Return is usually fairly even or slightly behind inflation.

N.O.W. (Negotiable Orders of Withdrawal) Account. Most checking accounts are called N.O.W. accounts. Many have per check charges and a monthly service charge. Those charges are often waived if a minimum daily balance is maintained. Some offer interest if a higher minimum balance is maintained.

This is a good account from which to operate your budget checking account. You should be able to maintain the minimum balance for free or reduced checking. This gives you the flexibility to issue as many checks as you need to maintain your budget.

Most of these accounts provide an ATM (Automatic Teller Machine) Card, which can be used at your bank or other banks around the country for making deposits or accessing cash. Many banks charge a transaction fee each time you use an ATM. ATM's have been the downfall of many people because it is easy to access cash and easy to forget to record it.

Many banks offer a combination ATM/DEBIT CARD. Not only does it allow you to access cash from the automated teller machines, it can also be used like a credit card, with one major difference. The money is automatically deducted from your account and transferred to the vendor when a transaction is made. This has some pros and cons. It could quickly empty the checking account of someone who uses it like a credit card.

Minimum Investment: $100.

Yield: 5.25% compounded monthly.

Super N.O.W. Account. Similar to above. Requires a higher initial deposit and higher minimums which must be maintained. All Super N.O.W. accounts offer interest which is usually a higher rate than on a regular N.O.W. account. The interest often fluctuates based on some nationwide standard, like two percentage points lower than prime. It offers more services than a regular N.O.W. account. This is often a good place to transfer your budget checking account to if you can maintain the higher minimum balance for free services and interest.

Minimum Investment: $1000-2,500.

Yield: 5.25% compounded monthly.

Credit Unions. Usually you have to belong to a particular group or union to participate in these. They generally offer both savings and checking at rates higher than the bank.

Minimum Investment: $50-100.

Yield: Varies, 2 to 3 percentage points higher than the bank.

United States EE Savings Bonds. These are bonds which you purchase through your local bank. You place an order and receive a check type receipt. The actual bond is sent to you later. They are sold in various denominations ($50, $75, $100, $200, $500, $1,000, $5,000 and $10,000). They cost half the face value of the bond ($25, $37.50, $50, $100, $250, $500, $2,500 and $5,000). The face value is what the bond is worth upon maturity at the end of 10 years and two months.

The EE Bonds can be redeemed between 6 months and a year after you purchase them for the amount you paid for the bond, plus 5.5% interest. The rate of interest raises the longer you hold the bonds. A minimum rate is guaranteed but the rate can go higher depending on the rate offered for marketable treasury securities.

The interest earned is exempt from state and local tax. No federal tax is due until the bond is redeemed. These bonds cannot be transferred, sold or used as collateral. You must redeem them if you need the cash.

Minimum Investment: $25.

Yield: 5.5% simple interest for 6 mo.-1 year.

C.D.s (Certificates of Deposit). These are issued by banks and offer you a higher rate of return than you get with your savings or N.O.W. account. They stipulate that you do not access the funds until a specific term is over. Terms can range for 30 days to a number of years.

A penalty is assessed, which is deducted from the interest you earn, if you redeem the certificate before its maturity date.

These are a very good place to put savings you know you will not need to access for the term of the certificate.

Minimum Investment: $500-1,000.

Yield: Slightly higher than regular savings and N.O.W. Accounts. Some are compounded monthly, many offer only simple interest.

Money Market Deposit Accounts. These are offered by banks and often provide a higher interest rate than N.O.W.s. They usually limit the amount of transactions you can conduct per month. Some limit it to three or five checks per month. This is a good place to keep a portion of your savings accessible, while providing a good rate of return. This is not a good account for your budget checking account because of the limit on transactions. You can write one check to clear out your account if you need the funds.

Minimum Investment: $1,000-5,000.

Yield: Usually .25% to .5% higher than N.O.W. accounts. Varies greatly from institution to institution.

Money Market Mutual Funds. These mutual funds invest only in liquid assets. Generally they offer limited check-writing privileges. They offer fairly consistent higher returns because of the diversity of investments they represent.

Usually offered by investment companies which offer a family of different mutual funds. That often provides the flexibility to transfer savings to other funds.

Minimum Investment: $250-1,000.

Yield: Varies. Often higher than N.O.W.s, similar to money market deposit accounts.

Treasury Bills. These are short-term notes backed by the federal government and are available for terms of 91 days, 182 days, and 52 weeks. They are considered a very stable investment.

Treasuries are exempt from state and local tax but not federal tax. You submit a bid to the government to purchase these at weekly auctions held by the government. Treasury bills, notes, and bonds (see the other sections) are all sold by the government at auction. Your bid (called a *tender*) must be accompanied by full payment for the face value of the treasury note. Your bid may be competitive or noncompetitive. If it is competitive, you state the interest rate you want, written out to two decimal points (i.e., 8.75%). If you want to place a noncompetitive bid, you agree to accept the average of the noncompetitive bids. This is the best way for the small investor.

A form with the following information should accompany your bid: your name, address and telephone number; your Social

Security number; the amount, type and length of maturity you want to purchase; the name in which you want it registered; the names and Social Security numbers if its a trust for minors; your signature; your payment; indicate if it is competitive or noncompetitive; and include a completed IRS W-9 form.

Bids should be mailed to: Bureau of Public Debt, Securities Transaction Branch, Room 2134, Main Treasury, Washington, D.C. 20226, or mail it to the Federal Reserve Bank in your area.

Notice of auctions are announced in the *Wall Street Journal* or can be secured by calling your local Federal Reserve Bank.

Minimum Investment: $10,000.

Yield: Usually higher than all the above.

Mutual Funds. Mutual funds open up a whole world of investment opportunities to the small or large investor. A person does not have to be very knowledgeable with the stock market or the ins and outs of investing to take advantage of the opportunities in mutual funds.

Mutual funds are pools of investments offered by investment companies who purchase a variety of investment vehicles, then pool them together to provide you the opportunity to have an experienced fund manager invest and reinvest the funds for your benefit.

The diversity of stocks which mutual funds invest in, often adds a greater standard of stability than you may experience by personally investing in one stock.

Mutual funds do not offer any guaranteed rate of return because it depends on the performance of their portfolio. Many funds have provided fairly consistent returns. Returns stated in ads, a prospectus or review are based on past performance and should be reviewed before investing your money. Various magazines and newsletters provide reviews of funds and identify what they believe are the best picks. These change from month to month.

Different funds invest in different types of companies and securities. Some categories of funds are listed below in increasing order of risk and rate of return:

Money Market Funds - invest in liquid assets like treasuries and notes which come due in less than a year. Provide a fairly reliable return.

Fixed Income Funds - provide a fairly stable yield for your dollar by investing in bonds and stocks with high dividends.

Income Funds - provide income by investing in conservative income-producing stocks and bonds, and some growth by investing in some stock of established companies.

Growth & Income Funds - provides growth by investing in stocks of established companies, and some income by investing in conservative income-producing stocks and bonds.

Growth Funds - provide long-term capital by investing in established companies. Subject to market swings.

Aggressive Growth Funds - provide maximum capital gains with a high risk factor by investing in speculative or new business ventures.

Some mutual funds specialize in a particular aspect of the investment market:

Municipal Bond Funds - invest primarily in bonds issued by government entities. Some are exempt from local, state, and federal taxes.

Sector Funds - concentrate their stocks in one industry like gold, chemicals, oil, utilities, health care, etc. These offer maximum capital gains but include big risks as they are dependent on one market.

International & Global Funds - invest in foreign stock and bond markets. This can experience tremendous shifts due to changes in the world economic or political structure. They often do not change at the same time as the U.S. market. Investors have seen some of the highest gains and losses with these funds.

Real Estate Funds - Invest in different types of mortgages and real estate companies.

You can buy a mutual fund direct from the investment firm which operates it. You are sent a prospectus (legal offering) which you are to read before you invest in the fund. Many investment firms offer a family of funds, which is advantageous if you want to invest a portion of your investment in various funds. It is often easier to transfer your money between funds if one fund in the family performs better than others and meets your objectives.

Mutual funds are classified as either "no-load" or "loaded."

Loaded Funds - you pay a fee for purchasing and/or selling shares.

No-Load - you do not pay a fee to buy or sell your shares.

Some investment advisors recommend you use exclusively no-load funds. Others argue loaded funds have loads because they are better performers and therefore can change the premium. Both sides of the argument have their good points.

Investment firms generally make their money through management fees, based on the profitability of the fund. You are not billed for these fees, they are deducted from the performance of the fund. Unlike a broker who gets a fee whether he makes a good investment for you or not, the fees earned by the mutual fund management company are often in direct proportion to the performance of the fund, therefore it is advantageous for the company to make a profit for you.

The value of your share is called the *net asset value* and is determined by dividing the value of the fund's cash and securities by the number of shares issued. That figure fluctuates daily.

Minimum Investment: $100-$1,000.

Yield: Not guaranteed. Some have consistently provided single digit returns while others have provided double digit returns. This fluctuates depending on the performance   of the fund in which you invest.

Intermediate-Term Investments

You can invest money you do not need to access for one to five years in intermediate-term investments, though many of these allow access sooner if needed. These are relatively liquid.

C.D.s (Certificates of Deposit). *See description under Short-Term Investments section above.*

Minimum Investment: $500-1,000.

Yield: Slightly higher than regular savings and N.O.W. Accounts. Some are compounded monthly, many offer only simple interest. The longer the term you are able to invest your money, the higher the yield.

Money Market Deposit Accounts. *See description under Short-Term Investments section above.*

Minimum Investment: $1,000-5,000.

Yield: Usually .25% to .5% higher than N.O.W. accounts. Varies greatly from institution to institution.

Money Market Mutual Funds. *See description under Short-Term Investments section above.*

Minimum Investment: $250-1,000.

Yield: Varies. Often higher than N.O.W.s, similar to money market deposit accounts.

United States EE Savings Bonds. *See description under Short-Term Investments section above.*

Minimum Investment: $25.

Yield: 5.5% simple interest for 6 mo.-1 year. Rates increase the longer you hold the bond. Rate fluctuates based on the rate offered on marketable treasury securities.

Mutual Funds. *See description under Short-Term Investments section above.*

Minimum Investment: $100-$1,000.

Yield: Not guaranteed. Fluctuates depending on the performance of the fund in which you invest.

Baby Bonds. Most bonds are offered in denomination of $1,000, but a few companies offer Baby Bonds in smaller denominations, similar to U.S. EE Savings Bonds. The purchase and sales fees are often higher than on larger bonds, but it gives the small investor the chance to invest in the bond market.

Minimum Investment: $25-100.

Yield: Varies, often higher than bank accounts.

Treasury Notes. These are debt obligations backed by the U.S. Government. They are bonds (though actual treasury bonds have terms of 10 to 30 years) with maturities ranging from one to ten years. This is considered one of the safest of all investment vehicles.

Unlike most other bonds, these do not have a *call feature* (see notes on Corporate Bonds, under Long-Term Investments section). It makes them a great investment if you buy them at 7.5% interest and interest rates drop to 5 percent.

See the section on Treasury Bills, under Short-Term Investments for information on how to purchase these.

Minimum Investment: $1,000 for those maturing in more than 4 years. $5,000 for those maturing in one to four years.

Yield: High Yield.

Tax Certificates. Some states and municipalities offer you the opportunity to buy past due property taxes. If the person does not pay their taxes for a certain number of years, the property becomes yours. If they pay their taxes, they usually have to pay you the going rate of interest plus a couple of percentage points. This debt becomes a priority lien on the property.

Minimum Investment: Varies.

Yield: High. Even higher if the person does not pay their taxes and the property becomes yours.

Limited Partnerships. You become a limited partner in an undertaking, assuming both liability and profitability in the project. A *General Partner* operates and manages the project. Usually the limit of liability is your capital investment. You participate in the capital gains, income and tax benefits from the project.

There are a variety of limited partnerships ranging from real estate, oil and gas, entertainment, and research and development. This is not liquid investment.

Minimum Investment: $5,000-25,000.

Yield: Varies. Could be very high, could be stable, or could be a loss.

Long-Term Investments

These are places where you can invest money you do not need to access for five years or more, though many of these can be accessed sooner. You should seek long-term security from these investments. These generally are not very liquid.

Real Estate. Real Estate is often viewed as an investment. During some markets money can be made in real estate with intermediate investments, but generally it takes five or more years for a property to *appreciate* (increase in value) to a point where it offsets the transaction costs involved.

The key to a good real estate investment is location. A property in a dying neighborhood will appreciate more slowly than one in a growing neighborhood. Some properties purchased at below market prices in a dying neighborhood, can be revived, and may be a good investment.

Minimum Investment: Varies.

Yield: For the long haul, most real estate appreciates. Depends on location, condition of the property and the economy.

Investment Quality Rare Coins & Art. Various collectables have outpaced other investments with high returns, especially quality rare coins and art. The value of a collectable is dependent on the willingness of someone to pay the price. Often, collectibles are sold at auction or bid. It takes much wisdom and advice to make a good investment in this area.

Minimum Investment: Varies.

Yield: Steady Increase.

IRA (Individual Retirement Account). A wide range of investment vehicles can be used as an individual retirement account. You determine what you want to be part of your IRA.

The government sets a limit as to who can invest in an IRA and how much they can invest each year. Check with your employer to see if you qualify.

You can have many different IRAs as long as you do not exceed the limits you are allowed to deposit in them for each calendar year. A good strategy is to have a few different IRAs or to have your IRA with a family of funds.

You may deduct the amount you invest from your income on your taxes. You do not pay income taxes on it until you withdraw it when you retire, when theoretically you will be in a lower tax bracket. You may start to withdraw money from your IRA starting as early as age 59 1/2 but starting no later than age 70 1/2. If you deposit $2,000 in an IRA and you are in a 25% tax bracket, you would immediately be saving $500 in taxes.

You may withdraw your funds from an IRA before you retire, but you must record it as income for the year it's withdrawn and pay a 10% penalty on the principal. If you have had your funds in an IRA and have earned more than 10% interest and need the funds, though it is not advisable to withdraw them, you will not suffer any great loss.

Minimum Investment: $50-1,000.

Yield: You determine it by the funds in which you invest.

Keough (Self-employed). A self-managed retirement fund, similar to I.R.A.s, for self-employed people or employees of unincorporated businesses. The amount of money you are allowed to invest is much higher than with an IRA, up to to 25 % of your net income. You can invest these funds in a wide variety of investment vehicles.

Minimum Investment: $50-1,000.

Yield: You determine the yield by the funds you invest in.

Annuities. A contract usually sold by insurance companies which provides a fixed or variable payment starting at a future date. Your funds accumulate tax deferred until withdrawn.

Minimum Investment: Varies.

Yield: Varies.

Zero Coupon Bonds. These are bonds stripped of their interest coupons and sold at below their face value. They can be sold before they mature, but their value is the face value of the bond at maturity. These are often used to finance a child's education or for retirement. You may buy a Zero, such as a $1,000 bond, which will mature in 20 years, for $100.

Even though you do not receive the tax until the bond matures, the IRS taxes you on the increase in the value of the bond each year. You can avoid that with tax-free zeros.

There are various types of Zeros:

Corporate Zeros - issued by corporations. Backed by faith in the company.

Treasury Zeros - offered by brokerage firms. They buy treasury bonds and clip off the semiannual interest coupons. You get the $1,000 face value upon maturity.

Tax-Exempt Zeros - from municipalities. Usually offer a lower return because their interest is tax exempt.

Zero Coupon C.D.s - offered by large banks. The interest is stripped off and you get the face value of the C.D. upon maturity.

Zero Mortgages - offered by large banks or mortgage companies. You receive the face value of the mortgage upon maturity.

Minimum Investment: $100+

Yield: Good

Corporate Bonds. A bond is an interest-bearing security which requires the issuer to pay the purchaser a specific amount of interest at specific periods, as well as the principal amount of the bond at its maturity. There are no ownership privileges in the company, like shareholders have. You simply own a security.

There are various types of bond terms to understand.

Bearer Bonds - you present the bond coupons and are paid the interest.

Secured Bonds - bonds which are backed by some particular collateral, which can be sold to make the bond payments, if needed.

Debenture Bonds - unsecured bonds backed only by faith in the company which issues them.

Convertible Bonds - these give the bond-holder the right to exchange the bond for other securities at a future date.

Junk Bonds - speculative bonds with ratings below BB. They usually pay higher yields but are very volatile and involve high risk because the companies issuing them usually do not have established track records.

Though a bond may be secure and the interest and face value may be paid upon maturity, the resale value of a bond during its life fluctuates depending on changes in market interest rates.

Most bonds have a *call feature*, which allows the issuing company to redeem the bond before maturity. They usually do this if interest rates drop much below the rate the bond was issued for. Treasury notes are not callable.

Bonds are rated by various financial services which analyze the bonds' strength and performance. Ratings range from AAA (highly unlikely to default) to D (in default).

Minimum Investment: $1,000.

Yield: Good.

Municipal Bonds. These are bonds issued by a government entity to either construct something or to help offset their debt. It is dependent on the strength of the municipality issuing the bonds. Usually the income is earned tax-free. These bonds are exempt from federal income taxes and from state or local taxes if they are from the state in which you live.

Minimum Investment: $1,000-2,500.

Yield: Good.

Mutual Funds. *See description under Short-Term Investments section above.*

Minimum Investment: $100-$1,000.

Yield: Not guaranteed. Fluctuates depending on the performance of the fund.

Precious Metals. Keeping part of an investment portfolio in precious metals like gold, silver, and platinum has been a practice observed by many people for a number of years. One problem with precious metals is that their value fluctuates so much. What may be a good investment today could be a bad investment tomorrow.

Minimum Investment: $25-$1,000.

Yield: Varies a lot. Very high highs and very low lows.

Treasury Bonds. These are long-term debt securities backed by the U.S. Government. Considered a stable investment, they mature from 10 to 30 years. If you can lock in a high rate of interest and interest rates drop, these are an excellent investment, unless the government fails.

See the section on Treasury Bills, under Short-Term Investments for information on how to purchase these and the section on Treasury Notes under Intermediate Investments.

Minimum Investment: $1,000.

Yield: Higher than banks offer.

Stocks. Stock provides you ownership in a corporation's profits and assets through the shares you own. Stock ownership usually provides you a vote in the election of the company's board of directors and a say in other matters brought before the shareholders.

There are many, many different types of stock. Because of the complexities of the stock market, one must be careful to understand what they are buying and how it operates.

As a company sees an increase in earnings it can pay its stock holders a dividend, usually annually. Values of stock fluctuates throughout the year as it is sold on the stock market. It is normal for most stocks to go up and down in price. A better stock will grow in value in the course of a year.

Some people use the investment strategy of buying stocks when their prices are down and selling them when the prices rise again.

Stocks have to bought through a broker and are subject to brokers fees, which you pay both when you buy and sell.

For the small investor a discount broker is probably best to use. Rates and services vary tremendously from one broker to another. Many discount brokers do not provide advice, they simply buy and sell what you tell them to.

Minimum Investment: Varies, $1,000-5,000.

Yield: Varies according to the performance of the stock.